USE THIS BOOK!

D1298665

USE THIS BOOK!

THE ONLY BOOK YOU'LL EVER NEED

BY **MELISSA HECKSCHER**

DESIGNED BY **MICHAEL ROGALSKI**

QUIRK BOOKS
PHILADELPHIA

COPYRIGHT PAGE

USE THIS PAGE TO FIND USEFUL PUBLISHING INFORMATION ABOUT THIS BOOK.

CONTENTS

USE THIS PAGE TO LOCATE USEFUL SECTIONS IN THIS BOOK.

USEFUL PERFORATION INCLUDED WITH EVERY PAGE!

CONTENTS

USE THIS PAGE TO FIND USEFUL EXHIBITS WITHIN EACH SECTION. CHECK OFF ITEMS TO KEEP TRACK OF WHICH ONES YOU'VE USED.

USE THIS SIGN TO DISCOURAGE SMOKING IN YOUR HOME OR WORK-PLACE.

INSTRUCTIONS: CUT ALONG DOTTED LINES. HANG SIGN IN PROMINENTLY VISIBLE PLACE.

NO SMOKING

NO
SMOKING

USE THIS SIGN TO NOTIFY OTHERS OF ITEM(S) YOU WOULD LIKE TO SELL.

INSTRUCTIONS: CUT ALONG DOTTED LINES. HANG SIGN IN A PROMINENTLY VISIBLE PLACE.

USE THIS SIGN TO DISCOURAGE DRIVERS FROM PARKING IN A SPOT THAT YOU WOULD LIKE TO RESERVE.

INSTRUCTIONS: CUT ALONG DOTTED LINES. HANG SIGN IN FRONT OF THE AREA WHERE YOU WOULD LIKE TO PROHIBIT PARKING.

NO PARKING ANY TIME

USE THIS SIGN TO NOTIFY STRANGERS THAT YOUR DOG IS AGGRESSIVE. IF YOU DO NOT OWN A DOG, DISPLAY THIS SIGN TO DETER VISITORS.

INSTRUCTIONS: CUT ALONG DOTTED LINES. HANG ON THE FRONT DOOR, FACING THE OUTSIDE.

BEWARE OF DOG

USE THIS SIGN TO LET OTHERS KNOW YOU HAVE NOT ABANDONED YOUR CAR AND THAT YOU WILL BE BACK WHEN POSSIBLE.

INSTRUCTIONS: CUT ALONG DOTTED LINES. HANG SIGN ON YOUR CAR WINDSHIELD, FACING OUTSIDE.

WENT FOR HELP

WENT FOR HELP

USE THIS SIGN TO NOTIFY OTHERS THAT YOU WILL BE BACK SOON.

INSTRUCTIONS: CUT ALONG DOTTED LINES. HANG SIGN IN A WINDOW OR OTHER VISIBLE PLACE.

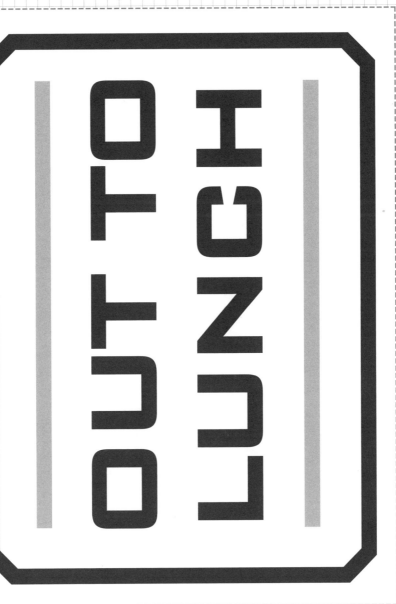

USE THIS SIGN TO LET OTHERS KNOW YOU WILL BE RIGHT BACK.

INSTRUCTIONS: CUT ALONG DOTTED LINES. HANG SIGN IN A VISIBLE PLACE.

BACK IN 5 MINUTES

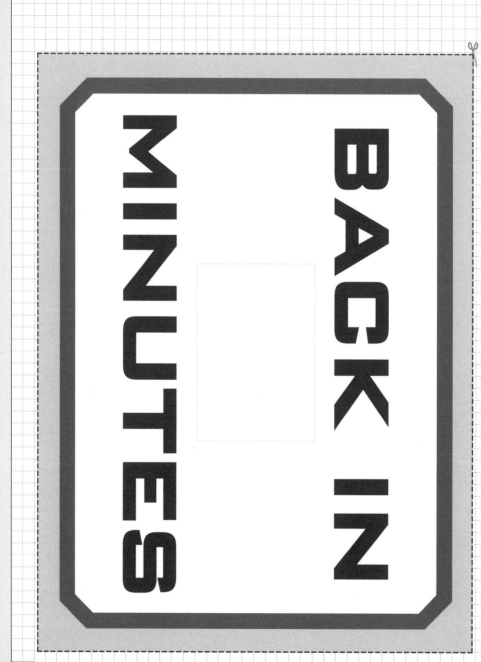

USE THIS SIGN TO LET OTHERS KNOW YOU DON'T WANT ANYONE DISTURBING YOU.

INSTRUCTIONS: CUT ALONG DOTTED LINES. HANG SIGN AROUND A DOORKNOB, FACING OUT.

PLEASE

DO
NOT
DISTURB

TAKE THIS SIGN WITH YOU WHEN YOU TRAVEL.

USE THIS SIGN TO LET THE CLEANING PERSON KNOW THAT YOU ARE READY FOR YOUR ROOM TO BE CLEANED.

INSTRUCTIONS: CUT ALONG DOTTED LINES. HANG SIGN AROUND A DOORKNOB, FACING OUT.

PLEASE
MAKE
UP
ROOM

TAKE THIS SIGN WITH YOU WHEN YOU TRAVEL.

USE THIS SIGN TO NOTIFY OUTSIDERS THAT THEY ARE NOT ALLOWED ON YOUR PROPERTY. THIS SIGN CAN BE USED IN CONJUNCTION WITH THE BEWARE OF DOG SIGN (SEE PAGE 11).

INSTRUCTIONS: CUT ALONG DOTTED LINES. HANG SIGN AT THE EDGE OF YOUR PROPERTY.

MAKE MULTIPLE COPIES OF THIS SIGN AND HANG THEM ON YOUR
PROPERTY'S PERIMETER.

NO TRESPASSING

USE THIS SIGN IF TRAPPED (AFTER A KIDNAPPING, FOR EXAMPLE) IN THE BACK OF A CAR, BUS, TRAIN, OR ANY OTHER PLACE WHERE YOU ARE UNABLE TO GET HELP BUT WHERE ANOTHER PERSON VIEWING THE SIGN MIGHT BE ABLE TO ASSIST YOU.

INSTRUCTIONS: CUT ALONG DOTTED LINES. HOLD UP TO A WINDOW SO OUTSIDERS CAN SEE THAT YOU NEED HELP.

CALL POLICE!

USE THIS SIGN TO NOTIFY PARKING ENFORCEMENT OFFICERS IF YOU'VE JUST PARKED IN A SPOT AT WHICH THE METER IS BROKEN.

INSTRUCTIONS: CUT ALONG DOTTED LINES AND AFFIX TO APPLICABLE PARKING METER. YOU MAY NEED TO USE TAPE TO AFFIX THE SIGN TO THE METER. IMPORTANT NOTE: LAWS VARY, BUT IN SOME LOCATIONS YOU MAY GET A TICKET EVEN IF THE METER IS BROKEN.

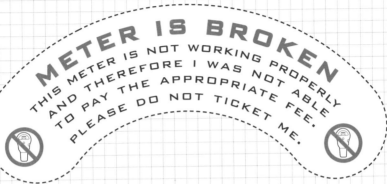

METER IS BROKEN
THIS METER IS NOT WORKING PROPERLY AND THEREFORE I WAS NOT ABLE TO PAY THE APPROPRIATE FEE. PLEASE DO NOT TICKET ME.

METER IS BROKEN
THIS METER IS NOT WORKING PROPERLY AND THEREFORE I WAS NOT ABLE TO PAY THE APPROPRIATE FEE. PLEASE DO NOT TICKET ME.

METER IS BROKEN
THIS METER IS NOT WORKING PROPERLY AND THEREFORE I WAS NOT ABLE TO PAY THE APPROPRIATE FEE. PLEASE DO NOT TICKET ME.

USE · THIS · SIGN

USE · THIS · SIGN

USE · THIS · SIGN

USE THIS CARD TO FAMILIARIZE YOURSELF WITH AIRLINE SAFETY.

INSTRUCTIONS: DETACH PAGE AND KEEP WITH YOU IN YOUR TRAVELS.

HOW TO EVACUATE A PLANE

USEFUL AIR TRAVEL TIPS

- DO NOT PACK OR BRING PROHIBITED ITEMS TO THE AIRPORT SUCH AS EXPLOSIVES, WEAPONS, OR "DUAL USE ITEMS" (THINGS THAT COULD BE CONSIDERED DANGEROUS, LIKE NAIL CLIPPERS, MATCHES, LIGHTERS, SCISSORS, AND BOX CUTTERS).
- PLACE JEWELRY, CASH, AND LAPTOP COMPUTERS IN CARRY-ON BAGGAGE ONLY.
- AVOID WEARING CLOTHING OR JEWELRY THAT CONTAINS METAL.
- AVOID WEARING SHOES THAT CONTAIN METAL OR HAVE THICK SOLES OR HEELS.
- PUT ALL UNDEVELOPED FILM AND CAMERAS IN YOUR CARRY-ON BAGGAGE. CHECKED BAGGAGE SCREENING EQUIPMENT WILL DAMAGE UNDEVELOPED FILM.
- USE A TSA-RECOGNIZED LOCK IF YOU PLAN ON LOCKING YOUR BAGS.
- DO NOT PACK OR CARRY ON WRAPPED GIFTS. (THEY MIGHT HAVE TO BE OPENED BY SECURITY.)

PACK THESE THINGS IN YOUR CARRY-ON BAGGAGE:

- ID (LICENSE OR PASSPORT)
- NECESSARY MEDICATIONS
- CHANGE OF CLOTHES (IN CASE OF LOST BAGGAGE)
- MOBILE PHONES
- COMPUTERS
- CAMERAS
- HOUSE KEYS
- PDAS (PERSONAL DATA ASSISTANTS)
- LARGE AMOUNTS OF JEWELRY

AVOID JET LAG! FOLLOW THESE HELPFUL TIPS:

- GET PLENTY OF SLEEP BEFORE YOU LEAVE.
- AVOID ALCOHOL AND CAFFEINATED BEVERAGES WHILE ON BOARD. TRY TO LESSEN INTAKE ON THE DAY PRIOR TO DEPARTURE.
- EAT WELL-BALANCED MEALS BEFORE AND DURING YOUR VACATION.
- EXERCISE ON THE DAYS PRIOR TO YOUR DEPARTURE.
- DRINK PLENTY OF WATER BEFORE AND DURING YOUR FLIGHT.
- GET USED TO YOUR NEW TIME ZONE BY PRACTICING LOCAL MEAL AND BEDTIME SCHEDULES.

WARNINGS!

- IT'S DANGEROUS TO FLY WITHIN 24 HOURS OF SCUBA DIVING. ASK YOUR DOCTOR OR DIVING AUTHORITIES FOR SPECIFIC GUIDELINES.
- AVOID BLOOD CLOTS IN YOUR LEGS, WHICH CAN BE FATAL: EXERCISE WHILE ON BOARD BY STRETCHING CALF MUSCLES AND TAKING PERIODIC WALKS UP AND DOWN THE AISLES.

USE THIS CHART TO HELP YOU FIND WATER IN DRY CLIMATES.

INSTRUCTIONS: DETACH PAGE AND CARRY IT IN YOUR BACKPACK. REMEMBER, WATER IS MORE IMPORTANT THAN FOOD WHEN GIVEN THE CHOICE.

HOW TO FIND WATER IN THE DESERT

LOOK FOR ANIMALS. ANIMALS NEED A WATER SOURCE TO SURVIVE, AND THEY WON'T STRAY TOO FAR FROM IT. PARTICULARLY WATCH FOR BIRD ACTIVITY AT SUNRISE OR SUNSET, AS BIRDS CONGREGATE NEAR WATER SOURCES AT THESE TIMES.

DIG FOR WATER. DRY CREEK BEDS MAY HAVE SOME WATER BELOW GROUND.

GATHER DEW. SMALL AMOUNTS OF DEW MIGHT COLLECT ON GREENERY, STONES, OR METAL SURFACES. WIPE OFF THESE SURFACES WITH A CLOTH AND WRING THE CLOTH INTO A CUP (MAKE YOUR OWN ON PAGE 193). WAKE UP EARLY TO DO THIS, AS DEW DRIES AN HOUR AFTER SUNRISE.

FOLD ▶

MAKE A RAIN CATCHER BEFORE A STORM. SET CUPS OUT, OR MAKE A CUP WITH HEAVY PAPER (SEE PAGE 193). FILL AS MANY CUPS AS POSSIBLE.

NOTE: DO NOT CUT OPEN CACTI; THERE IS NO WATER INSIDE THEM, AS SOME MYTHS PURPORT, AND THE MILK IN SOME CACTI MAY BE HARMFUL IF INGESTED.

OTHER TIPS:

* BREATHE THROUGH YOUR NOSE TO PREVENT WATER LOSS.

* BEFORE YOU DRINK YOUR WATER, LET IT SIT FOR AT LEAST 30 MINUTES. ANY CONTAMINANTS WILL SINK TO THE BOTTOM, AND THE CLEANEST DRINKING WATER WILL BE ON TOP.

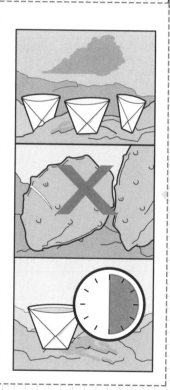

USE THIS GUIDE TO HELP IF YOU OR A FRIEND IS BITTEN BY A VENOMOUS SNAKE.

INSTRUCTIONS: DETACH PAGE AND KEEP WITH YOU WHEN TRAVELING IN AREAS WITH SNAKES. **NOTE:** IT'S ALWAYS BEST TO GET TO A HOSPITAL IMMEDIATELY IF BITTEN BY A POISONOUS SNAKE; THE INSTRUCTIONS BELOW ASSUME YOU'RE IN AN ISOLATED AREA.

HOW TO TREAT A VENOMOUS SNAKE BITE

1. IF YOU HAVE A MOBILE PHONE AND HAVE SERVICE, CALL EMERGENCY SERVICES TO REPORT YOUR LOCATION.

2. TIE A BANDAGE (OR A STRIP OF FABRIC) A FEW FINGERS' WIDTH ABOVE THE BITE TO SLOW DISTRIBUTION OF VENOM. THE BANDAGE SHOULD NOT CUT OFF CIRCULATION; A GOOD RULE OF THUMB IS THAT YOU SHOULD BE ABLE TO EASILY SLIDE A FINGER BENEATH THE BANDAGE.

3. IF HELP IS ON THE WAY, KEEP THE VICTIM STILL, POSITION-ING THE LIMB THAT WAS BITTEN BELOW THE LEVEL OF THE HEART. IF YOU MUST MOVE, DO SO SLOWLY AND TRY TO STAY RELAXED; A RAPID PULSE RATE WILL ONLY SPREAD THE POISON FASTER.

4. MONITOR THE VICTIM'S VITAL SIGNS—TEMPERATURE, PULSE, RATE OF BREATHING, BLOOD PRESSURE. IF THERE ARE SIGNS OF SHOCK (SUCH AS PALENESS), LAY THE VICTIM FLAT, RAISE THE FEET, AND COVER THE VICTIM WITH A BLANKET.

5. WHEN HELP HAS ARRIVED OR YOU HAVE REACHED A HOS-PITAL, DESCRIBE THE SNAKE TO THE PARAMEDIC SO THAT THE CORRECT ANTI-VENOM SERUM CAN BE ADMINISTERED.

DO NOT TRY TO "SUCK OUT" THE VENOM. THIS DOESN'T WORK AND IS MORE LIKELY TO POISON YOU THAN HELP THE VICTIM.

DO NOT PUT ICE ON THE WOUND.

DO NOT GIVE THE VICTIM ALCOHOLIC DRINKS.

BEFORE A STRIKE, A SNAKE WILL USUALLY DISPLAY A FEW WARNING SIGNS. THESE INCLUDE:
* BARING FANGS: OPENING THE MOUTH WIDE TO DISPLAY TEETH.
* MAKING A WARNING NOISE: HISSING, SPITTING, RATTLING, SHAKING VEGETATION.
* GETTING INTO STRIKE POSITION: THIS IS THE CLASSIC S SHAPE. MOST SNAKES WILL MAKE A FEW FALSE STRIKES WITH THEIR MOUTHS CLOSED BEFORE STRIKING PREY.

COMMON VENOMOUS SNAKES

RATTLESNAKE: MEDIUM-SIZED SNAKES, ABOUT 2 TO 5 FEET (.6–1.5 M) LONG THAT ARE FOUND AROUND THE WORLD IN GRASSLANDS, DESERTS, WOODLANDS, AND CANYONS. COLORS VARY, BUT ALL RATTLESNAKES HAVE OVAL, SQUARE, OR DIAMOND-SHAPED MARKINGS ON THEIR BACKS, AND ALL HAVE A RATTLE.
HABITAT: WORLDWIDE.

COPPERHEAD: SMALL SNAKES, ABOUT 22 TO 36 INCHES (56–91 CM) LONG, WITH RED HOURGLASS-SHAPED BANDS ACROSS THEIR BACKS. THEY CAN APPEAR PINKISH IN TINT, WITH A RUST-COLORED TRIANGULAR HEAD AND ELLIPTICAL PUPILS. THEY LOVE LIVING IN BRUSH OR WOOD PILES.
HABITAT: WORLDWIDE, PARTICULARLY WOODED AREAS OF NORTH AMERICA AND AUSTRALIA.

EGYPTIAN COBRA: LARGE SNAKES, UP TO 18 FEET (5.5 M) LONG, WITH YELLOW, DARK BROWN, OR BLACK UNIFORM BODIES AND BROWN CROSSBANDS. THEIR HEADS ARE SOMETIMES BLACK. ONCE AROUSED OR THREATENED, THEY WILL ATTACK AND CONTINUE ATTACKING UNTIL THEY FEEL THEY CAN ESCAPE.
HABITAT: AFRICA, IRAQ, SYRIA, SAUDI ARABIA.

COTTONMOUTH (WATER MOCCASIN): SMALL SNAKES, ABOUT 20 TO 48 INCHES (51–122 CM) LONG, GENERALLY DARK BROWN, OLIVE GREEN, OR ALMOST SOLID BLACK IN COLOR. THEY HAVE DARK BANDS AROUND THEIR BODIES. THE NAME "COTTONMOUTH" COMES FROM THE WHITISH INTERIOR OF THEIR MOUTHS, WHICH THEY DISPLAY WHEN THREATENED.
HABITAT: SOUTHEASTERN HALF OF THE UNITED STATES IN WOODED WETLANDS, SWAMPS, MARSHES, RIVERS, PONDS, AND STREAMS.

CORAL SNAKE: SLENDER SNAKES, ABOUT 30 INCHES (76 CM) LONG, WITH A SMALL HEAD AND ROUND PUPILS. THEIR DISTINCTIVE PATTERN IS A BROAD BLACK RING, A NARROW YELLOW RING, AND A BROAD RED RING, WITH THE RED RINGS ALWAYS BORDERED BY THE YELLOW RINGS.
HABITAT: THERE ARE ABOUT 30 SPECIES FOUND THROUGH-OUT THE WORLD; THEY ARE RARELY SEEN BECAUSE OF THEIR TENDENCY TO BURROW UNDERGROUND.

USE THIS CHART WHEN SOMEONE NEAR YOU IS CHOKING. THESE INSTRUCTIONS COULD SAVE A LIFE.

INSTRUCTIONS: DETACH CHART ALONG DOTTED LINES AND KEEP IN THE KITCHEN OR EATING AREA, WHERE CHOKING INCIDENTS ARE MOST LIKELY TO OCCUR.

THE HEIMLICH MANEUVER FOR AN ADULT

WHEN THE VICTIM IS CONSCIOUS:

1. STAND BEHIND THE VICTIM AND WRAP YOUR ARMS AROUND HIS OR HER WAIST.

2. MAKE A FIST AND PLACE THE THUMB SIDE AGAINST THE VICTIM'S UPPER ABDOMEN, BELOW THE RIB CAGE AND ABOVE THE NAVEL.

3. GRASP YOUR FIST WITH YOUR OTHER HAND AND PRESS INTO THE UPPER ABDOMEN WITH A QUICK UPWARD THRUST.

4. REPEAT UNTIL THE OBJECT IS EXPELLED.

WHEN THE VICTIM IS UNCONSCIOUS:

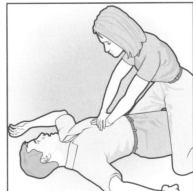

1. PLACE THE VICTIM ON HIS OR HER BACK. KNEEL ASTRIDE THE VICTIM'S HIPS.

2. WITH ONE OF YOUR HANDS ON TOP OF THE OTHER, PLACE THE HEEL OF YOUR BOTTOM HAND ON THE UPPER ABDOMEN, BELOW THE RIB CAGE AND ABOVE THE NAVEL.

3. USING YOUR BODY WEIGHT, PRESS INTO THE VICTIM'S UPPER ABDOMEN WITH A QUICK UPWARD THRUST.

4. REPEAT UNTIL THE OBJECT IS EXPELLED. IF THE VICTIM HAS NOT RECOVERED, PROCEED WITH CPR. (SEE PAGE 37.)

WARNING: DO NOT SLAP THE VICTIM'S BACK—THIS COULD MAKE THINGS WORSE.

THE HEIMLICH MANEUVER FOR A CHILD

1. LAY THE CHILD DOWN, FACE UP, ON A FIRM SURFACE AND KNEEL OR STAND AT HIS OR HER FEET; YOU CAN ALSO HOLD THE INFANT ON YOUR LAP FACING AWAY FROM YOU.

2. PLACE THE MIDDLE AND INDEX FINGERS OF BOTH YOUR HANDS BELOW THE CHILD'S RIB CAGE AND ABOVE THE NAVEL.

3. PRESS INTO THE CHILD'S UPPER ABDOMEN WITH A QUICK UPWARD THRUST; BE VERY GENTLE, AND BE CAREFUL NOT TO SQUEEZE THE RIB CAGE.

4. REPEAT UNTIL THE OBJECT IS EXPELLED.

5. IF THE CHILD HAS NOT RECOVERED, PROCEED WITH CPR (PAGE 38). THE CHILD SHOULD SEE A DOCTOR AFTER RESCUE.

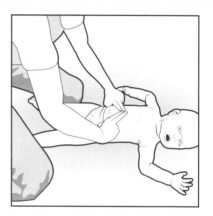

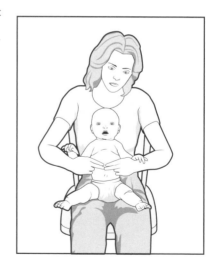

WARNING: DON'T SLAP THE CHILD'S BACK—IT COULD MAKE THINGS WORSE.

USE THIS CHART IF YOU SEE SOMEONE WHO APPEARS TO HAVE STOPPED BREATHING.

INSTRUCTIONS: DETACH ALONG DOTTED LINES AND CARRY WITH YOU AT ALL TIMES IN CASE OF EMERGENCY. CPR (CARDIOPULMONARY RESPIRATION) IS A COMBINATION OF RESCUE BREATHING (MOUTH-TO-MOUTH RESUSCITATION) AND CHEST COMPRESSIONS, BOTH DESIGNED TO BRING A PERSON'S HEART RATE AND BREATHING BACK TO NORMAL. **WARNING:** DO NOT ATTEMPT TO DO CPR UNLESS YOU ARE TOTALLY FAMILIAR WITH THE PROCEDURE.

CPR FOR AN ADULT

1. CALL EMERGENCY SERVICES SO THAT HELP IS ON ITS WAY.

2. POSITION THE VICTIM ON HIS OR HER BACK, BEING CAREFUL NOT TO TWIST THE HEAD, NECK, OR SPINE.

3. TILT THE HEAD BACK TO OPEN THE AIRWAY. CHECK TO SEE IF THE VICTIM IS BREATHING BY OBSERVING HIS OR HER CHEST FOR MOVEMENT OR BY LISTENING FOR BREATH IN THE LUNGS.

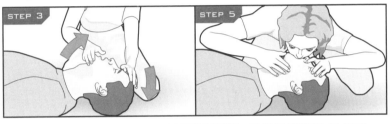

4. CHECK THE AIRWAY FOR OBSTRUCTIONS. IF THE VICTIM IS NOT BREATHING, CONTINUE TO STEP 5.

5. PINCH THE VICTIM'S NOSE AND COVER THE MOUTH WITH YOURS. BREATHE TWICE INTO THE MOUTH WITH FULL BREATHS.

6. CHECK PULSE FOR 10 SECONDS. IF THERE IS NO PULSE, CONTINUE TO STEP 7.

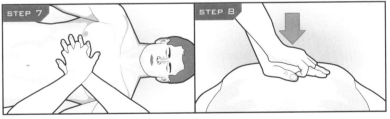

7. PLACE ONE HAND ON TOP OF THE OTHER AND THE HEEL OF THE BOTTOM HAND ON THE CENTER OF THE VICTIM'S CHEST, BETWEEN THE NIPPLES.

8. LOCK YOUR ELBOWS AND BEGIN FORCEFUL CHEST COMPRESSIONS AT A RATE OF 15 COMPRESSIONS FOR EVERY TWO BREATHS. THIS CIRCULATES BLOOD AND MAINTAINS BLOOD FLOW TO MAJOR ORGANS.

9. CHECK PULSE AFTER ONE MINUTE.

10. CONTINUE UNTIL HELP ARRIVES OR UNTIL THE VICTIM IS REVIVED.

CPR FOR A CHILD (AGE 12 MONTHS TO 8 YEARS)

THE CPR PROCEDURE FOR CHILDREN IS SIMILAR TO THE ONE USED FOR ADULTS; HOWEVER, COMPRESSIONS SHOULD BE CONSIDERABLY LESS FORCEFUL THAN THOSE USED ON ADULTS. DO NOT ATTEMPT CPR UNLESS YOU ARE COMPLETELY SURE OF WHAT YOU'RE DOING.

1. CALL EMERGENCY SERVICES SO THAT HELP IS ON THE WAY WHILE YOU ATTEMPT CPR.

2. POSITION THE CHILD ON HIS OR HER BACK, BEING CAREFUL NOT TO TWIST THE HEAD, NECK, OR SPINE.

3. TILT THE CHILD'S HEAD BACK TO OPEN THE AIRWAY. CHECK TO SEE IF THE CHILD IS BREATHING BY OBSERVING HIS OR HER CHEST FOR MOVEMENT OR BY LISTENING FOR BREATH IN THE LUNGS.

4. CHECK THE AIRWAY FOR OBSTRUCTIONS. IF THE VICTIM IS NOT BREATHING, CONTINUE TO STEP 5.

5. PINCH THE CHILD'S NOSE AND MAINTAIN AN OPEN AIRWAY AS YOU COVER HIS OR HER MOUTH WITH YOURS. GIVE TWO LONG, SLOW BREATHS, USING JUST ENOUGH AIR TO MOVE THE CHEST UP AND DOWN.

6. CHECK THE CHILD'S PULSE (AT THE NECK) FOR 10 SECONDS. IF THERE IS NO PULSE, CONTINUE TO STEP 7. IF THERE IS A PULSE BUT STILL NO BREATHING, CONTINUE RESCUE BREATHING ABOUT 1 BREATH EVERY 3 SECONDS.

7. POSITION YOUR HANDS TO BEGIN COMPRESSIONS: MOVE THE HEEL OF ONE HAND TWO FINGER WIDTHS ABOVE THE LOWER BREASTBONE (JUST BELOW THE IMAGINARY LINE BETWEEN THE TWO NIPPLES).

8. PLACE THE OTHER HAND ON TOP OF THE FIRST HAND, INTERLACING YOUR FINGERS. LEAN FORWARD SO YOUR SHOULDERS ARE OVER YOUR HANDS, THEN DO 5 COMPRESSIONS FOR EVERY ONE BREATH (NOTE: THIS IS DIFFERENT THAN FOR AN ADULT).

9. CONTINUE THE 5:1 COMPRESSIONS 12 TIMES, THEN CHECK PULSE AND BREATHING.

10. CONTINUE THIS CYCLE UNTIL THE CHILD'S CONDITION CHANGES, OR HELP ARRIVES.

USE THESE CARDS TO HELP TREAT BASIC AILMENTS.

INSTRUCTIONS: DETACH ALONG DOTTED LINES AND KEEP HANDY IN CASE OF AN ACCIDENT. WARNING: THIS IS NOT A SUBSTITUTE FOR PROFESSIONAL MEDICAL ATTENTION.

BASIC FIRST AID

SHOCK

SIGNS: LIGHTHEADEDNESS, CONFUSION, CLAMMY AND COLD SKIN, PALENESS, RAPID AND WEAK PULSE, THIRST, NAUSEA, VOMITING. LOSS OF CONSCIOUSNESS AND BLUE LIPS OR EARLOBES ARE LATE SIGNS OF SHOCK AND ARE VERY SERIOUS.

TREATMENT: IF THERE ARE NO HEAD OR CHEST INJURIES, LAY THE VICTIM ON HIS OR HER BACK SO THAT THE CHEST IS BELOW THE LEGS. KEEP THE VICTIM WARM.

MINOR BLEEDING

SIGNS: MINOR BLEEDING FROM AN OPEN CUT. WOUNDS WITH JAGGED EDGES OR THAT ARE CUT DEEPLY THROUGH THE SKIN, EXPOSING FAT OR MUSCLE, NEED MEDICAL ATTENTION AND STITCHES.

TREATMENT: MINOR CUTS USUALLY STOP BLEEDING ON THEIR OWN. IF NOT, APPLY GENTLE PRESSURE TO THE WOUND WITH A CLEAN CLOTH. IF BLEEDING DOES NOT STOP WITHIN 30 MINUTES, CONTACT A DOCTOR. CLEAN THE WOUND WITH WATER. (DO NOT USE SOAP, WHICH MAY AGGRAVATE THE WOUND.) APPLY AN ANTIBIOTIC CREAM ONCE THE WOUND IS DRY AND THE BLEEDING HAS STOPPED, TO HELP PREVENT INFECTION. NO MATTER HOW SMALL THE WOUND, ENSURE THAT THE VICTIM IS UP TO DATE ON TETANUS SHOTS (A NEW DOSE IS NEEDED EVERY 10 YEARS).

EYE INJURY

SIGNS: PAIN AND VISION OBSTRUCTION IN AFFECTED EYE.

TREATMENT: ATTEMPT TO FLUSH OUT THE FOREIGN BODY WITH RUNNING WATER OR EYE WASH (IF AVAILABLE). DO NOT TRY TO REMOVE FOREIGN BODIES WITH TOOLS (LIKE A FORCEPS). IF THE INJURY IS FROM CHEMICALS, RINSE OUT EYES THOROUGHLY, PLACE AN EYE PAD OVER THE AFFECTED EYE, AND SEEK MEDICAL ASSISTANCE.

BURNS

SIGNS: FIRST-DEGREE BURNS ARE CHARACTERIZED BY REDNESS WITH MILD SWELLING, PAIN, AND INCREASED SENSITIVITY TO HEAT; SECOND-DEGREE BURNS ARE CHARACTERIZED BY SWELLING AND BLISTERY FORMATIONS AND INCREASED PAIN, ESPECIALLY TO TOUCH OR TEMPERATURE CHANGES; THIRD-DEGREE BURNS ARE CHARACTERIZED BY HARD, DRY, LEATHERY SKIN OR DEAD TISSUE.

TREATMENT: MINOR BURNS, FIRST- OR SECOND-DEGREE UP TO 2 TO 3 INCHES (5–7.5 CM) IN DIAMETER, SHOULD BE TREATED BY COOLING THE AREA WITH COLD WATER AS QUICKLY AS POSSIBLE. SEVERE BURNS (THOSE WITH BLISTERS) SHOULD BE COOLED AND THE INJURED PERSON SHOULD BE TAKEN TO A DOCTOR. **DO NOT** TRY TO CLEAN THE WOUND OR REMOVE ANY CHARRED CLOTHING. FOR CHEMICAL BURNS, REMOVE THE CLOTHING AND WASH THE AREAS WITH COOL WATER FOR UP TO 20 MINUTES. SEEK MEDICAL ASSISTANCE IMMEDIATELY.

FOLD

SPRAINS AND STRAINS

SIGNS: SWELLING AND PAIN IN THE AFFECTED AREA.

TREATMENT: REST THE ARM OR LEG IN THE MOST COMFORTABLE POSITION POSSIBLE, AND APPLY AN ICE PACK COVERED IN CLOTH TO THE AREA. COMPRESS THE AREA USING BANDAGES. ELEVATE THE INJURED AREA ABOVE THE HEART TO PREVENT SWELLING.

FOLD

EMERGENCY KIT CHECKLIST

☐ STERILE ADHESIVE BANDAGES IN VARIOUS SIZES
☐ ASSORTED SIZES OF SAFETY PINS
☐ CLEANSING AGENT/SOAP
☐ LATEX GLOVES (2 PAIRS)
☐ SUNSCREEN
☐ STERILE GAUZE PADS (4–6 IN DIFFERENT SIZES)
☐ TRIANGULAR BANDAGES (3)
☐ NON-PRESCRIPTION DRUGS
☐ ANTISEPTIC
☐ STERILE ROLLER BANDAGES (3 ROLLS IN DIFFERENT SIZES)
☐ SCISSORS
☐ TWEEZERS
☐ NEEDLE
☐ MOISTENED TOWELETTES
☐ THERMOMETER
☐ TONGUE BLADES (2)
☐ TUBE OF PETROLEUM JELLY OR OTHER LUBRICANT

USE THIS CHART TO DETERMINE WHAT PLANTS MAY BE POISONOUS AND SHOULD NEVER BE INGESTED.

INSTRUCTIONS: DETACH CHART ALONG DOTTED LINES AND DISPLAY PROMINENTLY, OR TAKE ALONG ON HIKES. TEACH CHILDREN THE DANGERS OF THESE PLANTS.

POISONOUS PLANT GUIDE

HOUSEPLANTS

DIEFFENBACHIA (DUMB CANE), ELEPHANT EAR

TOXIC PART: ALL PARTS.

SYMPTOMS: PAINFUL IRRITATION TO THE MOUTH. CAN BE FATAL IF TONGUE SWELLS ENOUGH TO BLOCK AIRWAY TO THROAT.

HYACINTH, NARCISSUS, DAFFODIL

TOXIC PART: BULBS.

SYMPTOMS: NAUSEA, VOMITING, AND DIARRHEA. CAN BE FATAL, ESPECIALLY TO CHILDREN.

OLEANDER

TOXIC PART: LEAVES, FLOWERS, AND BRANCHES (POISONOUS EVEN IF USING BRANCHES AS SKEWERS TO ROAST MEAT).

SYMPTOMS: WEAKNESS, DIZZINESS, VOMITING OR NAUSEA, HEADACHES, RASH OR HIVES, CONFUSION, LOW BLOOD PRESSURE, IRREGULAR HEARTBEAT, AND DEATH. A SINGLE LEAF CAN KILL A CHILD.

ROSARY PEA, CASTOR BEAN

TOXIC PART: SEEDS.

SYMPTOMS: BURNING FEELING IN THE MOUTH, VOMITING, AND STOMACH PAINS. AMONG THE MOST POISONOUS PLANTS KNOWN TO HUMANS. A SINGLE ROSARY PEA OR ONE OR TWO CASTOR BEAN SEEDS CAN CAUSE DEATH FOR BOTH CHILDREN AND ADULTS.

FLOWER GARDEN PLANTS

AUTUMN CROCUS, STAR OF BETHLEHEM

TOXIC PART: BULB.

SYMPTOMS: VOMITING, NERVOUSNESS, ANXIETY, DEATH.

FOXGLOVE

TOXIC PART: LEAVES.

SYMPTOMS: NAUSEA, CONFUSION, SALIVATION, IRREGULAR HEARTBEAT AND PULSE IF INGESTED IN LARGE AMOUNTS, DEATH (RARE).

IRIS

TOXIC PART: UNDERGROUND STEMS.

SYMPTOMS: SEVERE DIGESTIVE UPSET, NAUSEA, DIARRHEA (NOT USUALLY FATAL).

LARKSPUR

TOXIC PART: YOUNG PLANT, SEEDS.

SYMPTOMS: UPSET STOMACH, ANXIETY, NERVOUSNESS, DEPRESSION, AND (IN RARE CASES) DEATH.

1 OF 4

POISONOUS PLANT GUIDE

FLOWER GARDEN PLANTS (CONTINUED)
LILY OF THE VALLEY
TOXIC PART: LEAVES AND FLOWERS, BULB.
SYMPTOMS: IRREGULAR HEARTBEAT AND PULSE, NAUSEA, MENTAL CONFUSION.

MONKSHOOD
TOXIC PART: FLESHY ROOTS.
SYMPTOMS: NAUSEA, NERVOUSNESS, ANXIETY, DEATH.

VEGETABLE GARDEN PLANTS
RHUBARB
TOXIC PART: LEAF BLADE.
SYMPTOMS: ABDOMINAL PAINS, VOMITING, CONVULSIONS, COMA. WITHOUT TREATMENT, DEATH OR SEVERE KIDNEY DAMAGE CAN OCCUR.

ORNAMENTAL PLANTS
DAPHNE
TOXIC PART: BERRIES.
SYMPTOMS: BURNING OR ULCERATION OF DIGESTIVE TRACT, VOMITING, DIARRHEA, DEATH (ESPECIALLY DANGEROUS TO CHILDREN).

GOLDEN CHAIN
TOXIC PART: SEEDS, PODS, FLOWERS.
SYMPTOMS: EXCITEMENT, SEVERE NAUSEA, CONVULSIONS, COMA IF LARGE AMOUNTS ARE EATEN, DEATH.

JASMINE
TOXIC PART: BERRIES.
SYMPTOMS: DIGESTIVE DISTURBANCE, NERVOUSNESS, DEATH.

LANTANA CAMARA (RED SAGE)
TOXIC PART: GREEN BERRIES.
SYMPTOMS: RANGE FROM MILD (GASTROINTESTINAL UPSET) TO SEVERE (CIRCULATORY COLLAPSE). CAN BE FATAL, ESPECIALLY TO CHILDREN.

LAUREL, RHODODENDRON, AZALEA
TOXIC PART: ENTIRE PLANT.
SYMPTOMS: NAUSEA, VOMITING, DEPRESSION, BREATHING DIFFICULTIES, COMA, DEATH.

POISONOUS PLANT GUIDE

ORNAMENTAL PLANTS (CONTINUED)
WISTERIA
TOXIC PART: SEEDS, PODS.
SYMPTOMS: DIGESTIVE UPSET (MILD TO SEVERE).

YEW
TOXIC PART: BERRIES, FOLIAGE.
SYMPTOMS: IF LARGE AMOUNTS ARE INGESTED, DEATH CAN OCCUR
SUDDENLY, WITHOUT SYMPTOMS. SMALLER AMOUNTS CAN CAUSE
TREMBLING AND DIFFICULTY BREATHING.

TREES AND SHRUBS
APPLES
TOXIC PART: SEEDS.
SYMPTOMS: NAUSEA AND STOMACH PAIN. CAN CAUSE DEATH IF
EATEN IN LARGE QUANTITIES.

BLACK LOCUST
TOXIC PART: BARK, SPROUTS, FOLIAGE.
SYMPTOMS: NAUSEA, WEAKNESS, DEPRESSION. SEEDS CAN BE
TOXIC TO CHILDREN.

ELDERBERRY
TOXIC PART: ALL PARTS (CHILDREN HAVE BEEN POISONED USING STEMS
AS BLOWGUNS).
SYMPTOMS: NAUSEA, DIGESTIVE UPSET.

OAK
TOXIC PART: FOLIAGE AND ACORNS.
SYMPTOMS: A FEW ACORNS PROBABLY WON'T HURT YOU, BUT
EATEN IN LARGE AMOUNTS, MAY CAUSE GRADUAL KIDNEY DAMAGE.

WILD CHERRIES
TOXIC PART: LEAVES AND PITS (THESE PARTS CONTAIN A COMPOUND
THAT RELEASES CYANIDE WHEN EATEN; SMALL AMOUNTS CAN BE TOLER-
ATED BY THE BODY, BUT VERY LARGE AMOUNTS CAN BE FATAL).
SYMPTOMS: NERVOUSNESS, STOMACHACHE, SHORTNESS OF
BREATH, SPASMS, COMA, DEATH (IF LARGE AMOUNTS ARE EATEN).

POISONOUS PLANT GUIDE

PLANTS IN WOODED AREAS
JACK-IN-THE-PULPIT
TOXIC PART: ALL PARTS.
SYMPTOMS: SEVERE BURNING IN MOUTH AND TONGUE.

MAYAPPLE
TOXIC PART: APPLE, FOLIAGE, ROOTS.
SYMPTOMS: VOMITING, GASTROENTERITIS, DIARRHEA. ROOTS ARE
    MOST DANGEROUS; RIPE FRUIT IS LEAST TOXIC.

MISTLETOE
TOXIC PART: BERRIES.
SYMPTOMS: ACUTE STOMACH AND INTESTINAL IRRITATION, DEATH.

MOONSEED
TOXIC PART: BERRIES (APPEARANCE RESEMBLES WILD GRAPES).
SYMPTOMS: INTESTINAL UPSET, DEATH.

WATER HEMLOCK
TOXIC PART: ALL PARTS.
SYMPTOMS: NERVOUSNESS AND TREMORS LEADING TO VIOLENT
    CONVULSIONS, DEATH.

PLANTS IN FIELDS
BUTTERCUPS
TOXIC PART: ALL PARTS.
SYMPTOMS: NAUSEA, VOMITING, SALIVATION, INTENSE IRRITATION
    OF DIGESTIVE SYSTEM, DEATH (RARE).

JIMSON WEED (THORN APPLE)
TOXIC PART: ALL PARTS.
SYMPTOMS: EXTREME THIRST, VISION DISTURBANCES, DELIRIUM,
    CONFUSION, COMA, DEATH.

NIGHTSHADE
TOXIC PART: ALL PARTS, ESPECIALLY UNRIPENED BERRY.
SYMPTOMS: DIGESTIVE UPSET, LOSS OF SENSATION, DEATH FROM
    PARALYSIS. RIPENED BERRIES ARE LESS TOXIC.

POISON HEMLOCK
TOXIC PART: ROOT (RESEMBLES WILD CARROT), FOLIAGE, SEEDS.
SYMPTOMS: WEAKENING OF MUSCLES, DEATH FROM PARALYSIS OF
    LUNGS. CAUSED SOCRATES'S DEATH.

USE THIS CARD SO THAT OTHERS CAN IDENTIFY YOU AND YOUR MEDICAL NEEDS IN AN EMERGENCY.

INSTRUCTIONS: CUT ALONG DOTTED LINES AND CARRY IN YOUR WALLET, PURSE, OR IN YOUR POCKET AT ALL TIMES.

NAME:_____

ADDRESS:_____

_____

PHONE NUMBER:_____ _____
                     (HOME)   (CELL)

EMERGENCY CONTACTS

NAME:_____

ADDRESS:_____

_____

PHONE NUMBER:_____ _____
                     (HOME)   (CELL)

NAME:_____

ADDRESS:_____

_____

PHONE NUMBER:_____ _____
                     (HOME)   (CELL)

NAME:_____

ADDRESS:_____

_____

PHONE NUMBER:_____ _____
                     (HOME)   (CELL)

EMERGENCY CONTACTS

NAME:_____

ADDRESS:_____

_____

PHONE NUMBER:_____ _____
                     (HOME)   (CELL)

NAME:_____

ADDRESS:_____

_____

PHONE NUMBER:_____ _____
                     (HOME)   (CELL)

THESE CARDS CAN SAVE YOUR LIFE. BE SURE TO FILL IN ALL FIELDS WITH A PERMANENT MARKER.

BLOOD TYPE:_____

PHYSICIANS:_____
_____
_____

MEDICAL CONDITIONS/ HISTORY:_____
_____
_____

MEDICATIONS (INCLUDE DOSAGE INFORMATION):_____
_____
_____

ALLERGIES:_____
_____
_____

OTHER INFORMATION:_____

BLOOD TYPE:_____

PHYSICIANS:_____
_____
_____

MEDICAL CONDITIONS/ HISTORY:_____
_____
_____

MEDICATIONS (INCLUDE DOSAGE INFORMATION):_____
_____
_____

ALLERGIES:_____
_____
_____

OTHER INFORMATION:_____

USE THIS BOOK TO KEEP TRACK OF PHONE NUMBERS AND ADDRESSES.

INSTRUCTIONS: CUT OUT PAGES ALONG DOTTED LINES AND STAPLE TOGETHER TO MAKE A SMALL BOOK.

WXYZ

CONTACTS

QRS

CD

MN

GH

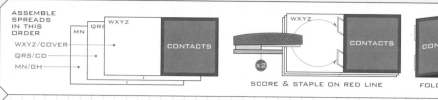

ASSEMBLE
SPREADS
IN THIS
ORDER

WXYZ/COVER
QRS/CD
MN/GH

SCORE & STAPLE ON RED LINE

FOLD & USE

FOLD & STAPLE ▼

AB

TUV

EF

OP

IJ

KL

USE THIS CALENDAR TO KEEP TRACK OF IMPORTANT DATES OVER A
TWELVE-MONTH PERIOD.

INSTRUCTIONS: FILL IN THE DAYS OF THE MONTHS. STICK THE
CALENDAR TO THE REFRIGERATOR OR A BULLETIN BOARD FOR EASY
REFERENCE.

	SUNDAY	MONDAY	TUESDAY	WEDNESDAY	THURSDAY	FRIDAY	SATURDAY
JANUARY							
FEBRUARY							
MARCH							
APRIL							
MAY							
JUNE							

	SUNDAY	MONDAY	TUESDAY	WEDNESDAY	THURSDAY	FRIDAY	SATURDAY
JULY							
AUGUST							
SEPTEMBER							
OCTOBER							
NOVEMBER							
DECEMBER							

USE THIS LIST TO KEEP TRACK OF GIFTS YOU BUY FOR FRIENDS AND FAMILY. THIS WAY, YOU'LL NEVER BUY SOMEONE THE SAME THING!

INSTRUCTIONS: DETACH PAGE AND KEEP WHERE CONVENIENT.

HOLIDAY GIFT LIST

NAME   GIFT

☐ _____   _____
☐ _____   _____
☐ _____   _____
☐ _____   _____
☐ _____   _____
☐ _____   _____
☐ _____   _____
☐ _____   _____
☐ _____   _____
☐ _____   _____
☐ _____   _____
☐ _____   _____
☐ _____   _____
☐ _____   _____
☐ _____   _____
☐ _____   _____
☐ _____   _____
☐ _____   _____
☐ _____   _____
☐ _____   _____
☐ _____   _____
☐ _____   _____
☐ _____   _____
☐ _____   _____
☐ _____   _____
☐ _____   _____
☐ _____   _____

CHECK OFF THE BOX ONCE YOU'VE PURCHASED THAT GIFT.

NAME   GIFT

☐
☐
☐
☐
☐
☐
☐
☐
☐
☐
☐
☐
☐
☐
☐
☐
☐
☐
☐
☐
☐
☐
☐
☐
☐
☐
☐
☐
☐

USE THIS LIST TO KEEP TRACK OF FAMILY AND FRIENDS' BIRTHDAYS.

INSTRUCTIONS: DETACH PAGE AND KEEP IT ON THE FRIDGE, IN YOUR WALLET, OR WHEREVER IS MOST CONVENIENT.

BIRTHDAY LIST

NAME	BIRTHDAY

BIRTHDAY LIST

NAME

BIRTHDAY

USE THIS LIST TO KEEP TRACK OF YOUR GROCERY NEEDS.

INSTRUCTIONS: MAKE COPIES OF THIS PAGE FOR FUTURE USE. LIST NEEDED GROCERIES ON IT, THEN TAKE IT WITH YOU TO THE GROCERY STORE.

GROCERY LIST

FRUITS AND VEGGIES	MEAT AND POULTRY
☐ _____	☐ _____
☐ _____	☐ _____
☐ _____	☐ _____
☐ _____	☐ _____
☐ _____	☐ _____
☐ _____	☐ _____
☐ _____	☐ _____
☐ _____	☐ _____
☐ _____	☐ _____
☐ _____	☐ _____
☐ _____	☐ _____
☐ _____	☐ _____
☐ _____	☐ _____
☐ _____	☐ _____
☐ _____	☐ _____
☐ _____	☐ _____
☐ _____	☐ _____
☐ _____	☐ _____
☐ _____	☐ _____
☐ _____	☐ _____
☐ _____	☐ _____
☐ _____	☐ _____
☐ _____	☐ _____
☐ _____	☐ _____
☐ _____	☐ _____
☐ _____	☐ _____
☐ _____	☐ _____

MAKE COPIES OF THIS LIST FOR FUTURE GROCERY VISITS.

FOLD ▼

PANTRY STAPLES

- [ ] _____
- [ ] _____
- [ ] _____
- [ ] _____
- [ ] _____
- [ ] _____
- [ ] _____
- [ ] _____
- [ ] _____
- [ ] _____
- [ ] _____
- [ ] _____
- [ ] _____
- [ ] _____
- [ ] _____
- [ ] _____
- [ ] _____
- [ ] _____
- [ ] _____
- [ ] _____
- [ ] _____
- [ ] _____
- [ ] _____
- [ ] _____
- [ ] _____
- [ ] _____
- [ ] _____

DAIRY AND BREADS

- [ ] _____
- [ ] _____
- [ ] _____
- [ ] _____
- [ ] _____
- [ ] _____
- [ ] _____
- [ ] _____
- [ ] _____
- [ ] _____
- [ ] _____
- [ ] _____
- [ ] _____
- [ ] _____

OTHER

- [ ] _____
- [ ] _____
- [ ] _____
- [ ] _____
- [ ] _____
- [ ] _____
- [ ] _____
- [ ] _____
- [ ] _____
- [ ] _____
- [ ] _____
- [ ] _____

USE THIS LIST TO KEEP TRACK OF ALL THE THINGS YOU HAVE TO DO.

INSTRUCTIONS: FILL IN LINES AS CALLED FOR. CHECK BOXES WHEN TASKS ARE COMPLETE.

TO DO LIST

TODAY:

- ☐ _____
- ☐ _____
- ☐ _____
- ☐ _____
- ☐ _____
- ☐ _____
- ☐ _____
- ☐ _____
- ☐ _____
- ☐ _____
- ☐ _____
- ☐ _____
- ☐ _____
- ☐ _____
- ☐ _____
- ☐ _____
- ☐ _____
- ☐ _____
- ☐ _____
- ☐ _____
- ☐ _____
- ☐ _____
- ☐ _____
- ☐ _____

TO DO LIST

TODAY:

- ☐ _____
- ☐ _____
- ☐ _____
- ☐ _____
- ☐ _____
- ☐ _____
- ☐ _____
- ☐ _____
- ☐ _____
- ☐ _____
- ☐ _____
- ☐ _____
- ☐ _____
- ☐ _____
- ☐ _____
- ☐ _____
- ☐ _____
- ☐ _____
- ☐ _____
- ☐ _____
- ☐ _____
- ☐ _____
- ☐ _____
- ☐ _____

REMEMBER THE MANTRA: DONE IS GOOD. KEEPING YOUR TO DO LIST CURRENT WILL GIVE YOU A GREAT DEAL OF SATISFACTION AS YOU CHECK THINGS OFF.

TO DO LIST

THIS MONTH:

- [ ] _____
- [ ] _____
- [ ] _____
- [ ] _____
- [ ] _____
- [ ] _____
- [ ] _____
- [ ] _____
- [ ] _____
- [ ] _____
- [ ] _____
- [ ] _____
- [ ] _____
- [ ] _____
- [ ] _____
- [ ] _____
- [ ] _____
- [ ] _____
- [ ] _____
- [ ] _____
- [ ] _____
- [ ] _____
- [ ] _____
- [ ] _____
- [ ] _____

TO DO LIST

THIS MONTH:

- [ ] _____
- [ ] _____
- [ ] _____
- [ ] _____
- [ ] _____
- [ ] _____
- [ ] _____
- [ ] _____
- [ ] _____
- [ ] _____
- [ ] _____
- [ ] _____
- [ ] _____
- [ ] _____
- [ ] _____
- [ ] _____
- [ ] _____
- [ ] _____
- [ ] _____
- [ ] _____
- [ ] _____
- [ ] _____
- [ ] _____
- [ ] _____
- [ ] _____

USE THIS TEMPLATE FOR KEEPING TRACK OF YOUR NEW YEAR'S RESOLUTIONS FROM YEAR TO YEAR.

INSTRUCTIONS: FILL IN THE APPROPRIATE YEAR AND YOUR RESOLUTIONS IN THE SPACE PROVIDED.

NEW YEAR'S RESOLUTIONS

YEAR _____

- ☐ _____
- ☐ _____
- ☐ _____
- ☐ _____
- ☐ _____
- ☐ _____
- ☐ _____

YEAR _____

- ☐ _____
- ☐ _____
- ☐ _____
- ☐ _____
- ☐ _____
- ☐ _____
- ☐ _____

YEAR _____

- ☐ _____
- ☐ _____
- ☐ _____
- ☐ _____
- ☐ _____
- ☐ _____
- ☐ _____

WHEN YOU MAKE NEXT YEAR'S RESOLUTIONS, LOOK BACK AT THE PREVIOUS YEAR'S. ASSESS HOW WELL YOU ACCOMPLISHED THEM.

NEW YEAR'S RESOLUTIONS

YEAR _____

☐ _____
☐ _____
☐ _____
☐ _____
☐ _____
☐ _____
☐ _____

YEAR _____

☐ _____
☐ _____
☐ _____
☐ _____
☐ _____
☐ _____
☐ _____

YEAR _____

☐ _____
☐ _____
☐ _____
☐ _____
☐ _____
☐ _____

USE THIS FORM TO TAKE DOWN MESSAGES FOR FAMILY OR ROOMMATES.

INSTRUCTIONS: CUT OUT THE INDIVIDUAL MESSAGES ALONG THE DOTTED LINES. LEAVE THE MESSAGE IN A CONSPICUOUS PLACE SO THAT THE MESSAGE GETS TO THE APPROPRIATE PERSON.

TO: _____
WHILE YOU WERE OUT
_____ CALLED
DATE _____ TIME _____
CALL BACK: _____ (PHONE)
FAX BACK: _____ (FAX)
MESSAGE: _____
_____
_____
SIGNED: _____

TO: _____
WHILE YOU WERE OUT
_____ CALLED
DATE _____ TIME _____
CALL BACK: _____ (PHONE)
FAX BACK: _____ (FAX)
MESSAGE: _____
_____
_____
SIGNED: _____

TO: _____
WHILE YOU WERE OUT
_____ CALLED
DATE _____ TIME _____
CALL BACK: _____ (PHONE)
FAX BACK: _____ (FAX)
MESSAGE: _____
_____
_____
SIGNED: _____

TO: _____
WHILE YOU WERE OUT
_____ CALLED
DATE _____ TIME _____
CALL BACK: _____ (PHONE)
FAX BACK: _____ (FAX)
MESSAGE: _____
_____
_____
SIGNED: _____

USE THIS STATIONERY TO WRITE NICE LETTERS.

INSTRUCTIONS: DETACH PAGE AND SEND IN AN ENVELOPE (SEE PAGE 65).

USE THIS ENVELOPE FOR SENDING A LETTER.

INSTRUCTIONS: CUT OUT ENVELOPE TEMPLATE AND FOLD AS INDICATED ON PAGE 68. USE TAPE OR GLUE TO ATTACH TO SECOND PANEL (PAGE 67).

USE THE OTHER SIDE OF THIS PAGE FOR THE OUTER FACE OF THE
ENVELOPE; FOLD SO THAT THE PRINTED RULES ARE INSIDE THE ENVELOPE.

GLUE HERE TO
SEAL ENVELOPE

FOLD

SEE REVERSE SIDE OF THIS PAGE FOR DETAILED ASSEMBLY INSTRUCTIONS.

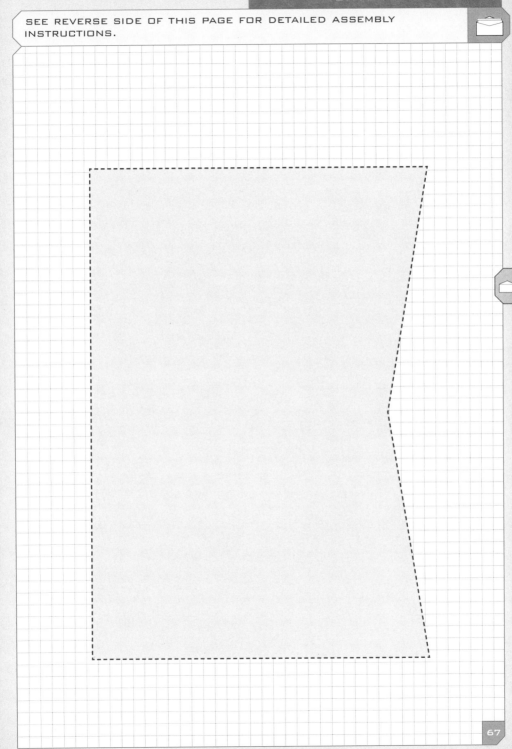

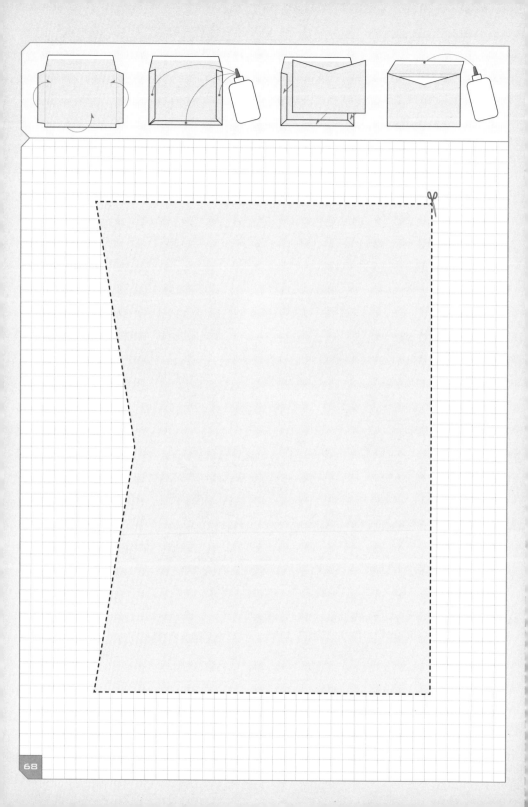

USE THIS GRAPH WHEN CALCULATING GEOMETRIC FIGURES, WORKING ON BLUEPRINTS, OR CHARTING A CRAFT PROJECT.

INSTRUCTIONS: CUT OUT GRAPH ALONG DOTTED LINE.

THE DARKER GRIDLINES ARE SPACED 10 BOXES APART SO THAT
MEASURING IS EASIER.

USE THIS PAPER FOR EASY NOTE-WRITING.

INSTRUCTIONS: CUT OUT PAGE ALONG DOTTED LINE.

DETACH PAGE AND CARRY WITH YOU WITH A PEN (NOT INCLUDED) SO BOTH
ARE HANDY WHEN YOU NEED THEM.

USE THIS KEYBOARD AS A TOOL FOR PRACTICING YOUR TYPING IF NO ACTUAL COMPUTER OR TYPEWRITER IS AVAILABLE.

INSTRUCTIONS: USE THIS "KEYBOARD" AS A GUIDE TO DETERMINE WHICH FINGERS GO WHERE. AS YOU IMPROVE, TRY CLOSING YOUR EYES AND FIGURING OUT THE LETTERS.

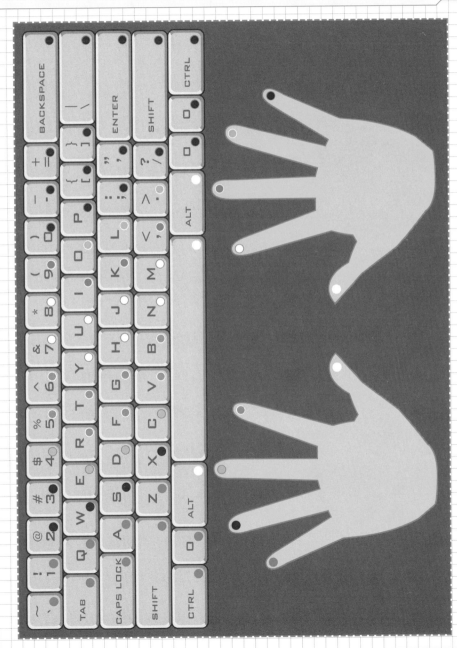

IMPROVE YOUR TYPING SKILLS

- TRY TO PRACTICE AT LEAST 15 MINUTES A DAY. A GOOD WAY TO PRACTICE IS TO COPY THINGS—LETTERS AND NEWSPAPER ARTICLES ARE GOOD EXAMPLES. TRANSCRIBING WHAT YOU HEAR ON TV IS ALSO A GOOD EXERCISE.

- DON'T LOOK AT THE KEYS. EVEN IF YOU MESS UP, IT'S BETTER TO LEARN THE CORRECT WAY THAN TO CHEAT.

- DON'T CORRECT YOURSELF. INSTEAD, LOOK AT THE MISTAKES YOU'RE MAKING AND IDENTIFY YOUR PROBLEM SPOTS.

- WORK ON YOUR PROBLEM SPOTS. (IF YOU ALWAYS MISS THE LETTER "Q," FOR EXAMPLE, TYPE AS MANY "Q" WORDS AS YOU CAN.)

PROPER POSTURE FOR TYPING:

- ADJUST YOUR CHAIR SO THAT YOUR BACK TOUCHES THE BACK OF THE CHAIR.

- REST YOUR FEET FIRMLY ON THE FLOOR.

- CENTER YOUR KEYBOARD IN FRONT OF YOUR MONITOR, NOT TO THE SIDE OR DIAGONAL FROM IT.

- THE KEYBOARD SHOULD BE CLOSE TO THE EDGE OF THE DESK, POSITIONED SO YOUR ARMS FALL AT YOUR SIDES AND YOUR WRISTS ARE STRAIGHT IN FRONT OF YOU WHILE TYPING OR USING THE MOUSE.

- USE A WRIST SUPPORT.

- KEEP FREQUENTLY USED ITEMS CLOSE BY SO YOU DON'T HAVE TO REACH FOR THINGS.

- DO PERIODIC WRIST, FINGER, AND HAND EXERCISES AND STRETCHES. TAKE BREAKS TO WALK AROUND AND STRETCH YOUR MUSCLES.

USE THESE BOOKMARKS TO KEEP YOUR PLACE IN YOUR READING MATERIAL.

INSTRUCTIONS: CUT BOOKMARKS OUT ALONG DOTTED LINES.

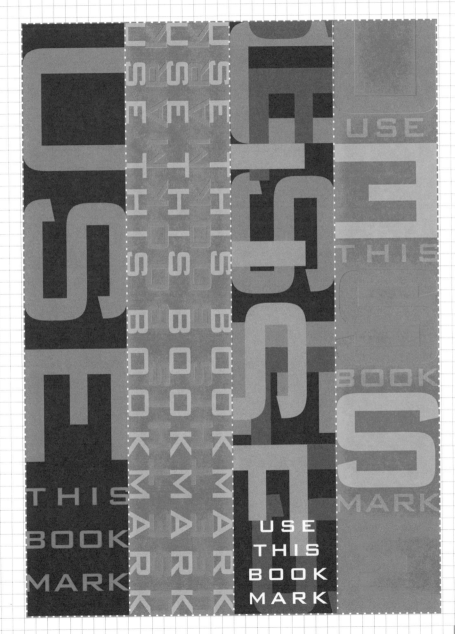

USE THIS BOOK MARK

USE THIS BOOK MARK

USE THIS GRID TO MEASURE SMALL ITEMS SUCH AS CARDS, PICTURES, OR FRAMES.

INSTRUCTIONS: LINE UP ITEM AT 0/0 MARK AND READ MEASUREMENTS ALONG VERTICAL (HEIGHT) AND HORIZONTAL (WIDTH) LINES.

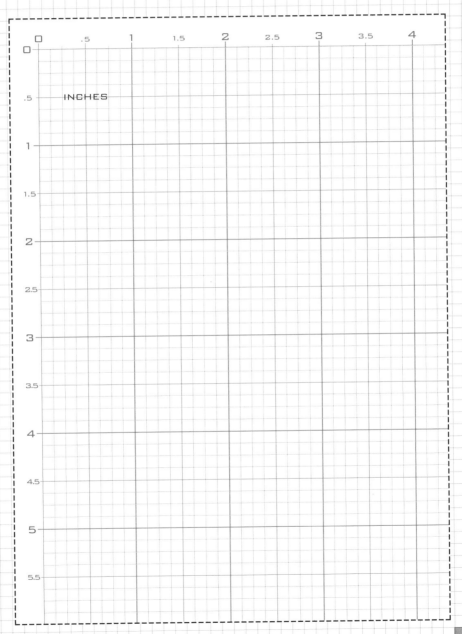

INCHES

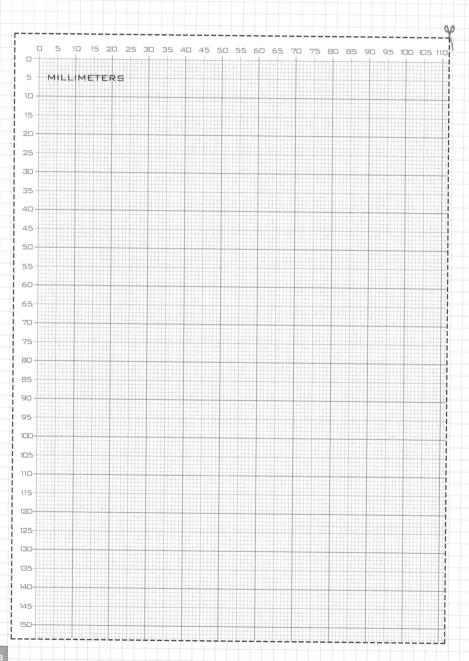

MILLIMETERS

USE THIS LIST TO HELP YOU AVOID COMMON SPELLING MISTAKES WHEN WRITING IMPORTANT LETTERS AND DOCUMENTS.

INSTRUCTIONS: DETACH PAGE, FOLD AS INDICATED, AND KEEP IN YOUR BACKPACK OR IN YOUR OFFICE DRAWER FOR EASY REFERENCE.

COMMONLY MISSPELLED WORDS

A LOT	BATTALION	CONTROVERSIAL	EXHILARATE
ABSENCE	BEGINNING	CONTROVERSY	EXISTENCE
ABUNDANCE	BENEFITED	CONVENIENT	EXPENSE
ACCEPTABLE	BISCUIT	CORRELATE	EXPERIENCE
ACCESSIBLE	BOUILLON	CORRESPONDENCE	EXPERIMENT
ACCIDENTALLY	BOUNDARY	COUNSELOR	EXPLANATION
ACCLAIM	BOURGEOIS	CRITICIZE	EXUBERANCE
ACCOMMODATE	BRITAIN	DECEIVE	FAHRENHEIT
ACCOMPLISH	BUSINESS	DEFENDANT	FAMILIAR
ACCORDION	CALENDAR	DEFERRED	FASCINATE
ACCUMULATE	CAMOUFLAGE	DEFINITELY	FEASIBLE
ACHIEVEMENT	CANTALOUPE	DEPENDENT	FICTITIOUS
ACQUAINTANCE	CATEGORY	DESCEND	FINANCIALLY
ACQUIRE	CEMETERY	DESPERATE	FLUORESCENT
ACQUITTED	CHANGEABLE	DEVELOP	FORCIBLY
ACROSS	CHARACTERISTIC	DEVELOPMENT	FOREIGN
ADVERTISEMENT	CHAUFFEUR	DILEMMA	FORESEE
AGGRAVATE	CHIEF	DISAPPEARANCE	FULFILL
ALLEGED	CIGARETTE	DISAPPOINT	GAUGE
AMATEUR	COLLECTIBLE	DISCIPLINE	GOVERNMENT
ANALYSIS	COLONEL	DISPENSABLE	GOVERNOR
ANALYZE	COLOSSAL	DISSATISFIED	GRAMMAR
ANNUAL	COMMITMENT	DOMINANT	GUARANTEE
APPARATUS	COMMITTEE	DORMITORY	GUERRILLA
APPARENT	COMPARATIVE	DRAWER	HANDKERCHIEF
APPEARANCE	COMPETENT	ECSTASY	HARASS
ARCTIC	COMPLETELY	EIGHTH	HEMORRHAGE
ARITHMETIC	CONCEDE	ELIGIBLE	HEROES
ASCEND	CONCEIVABLE	ELIMINATE	HOARSE
ATHEIST	CONDEMN	EMBARRASS	HYPOCRISY
ATTENDANCE	CONDESCEND	EMINENT	HYPOCRITE
AUXILIARY	CONSCIENCE	ENTIRELY	IDEALLY
BALLOON	CONSCIENTIOUS	EQUIPPED	IDIOSYNCRASY
BARBECUE	CONSCIOUS	EQUIVALENT	IGNORANCE
BARBITURATE	CONSENSUS	EXAGGERATE	IMMEDIATELY
BARGAIN	CONSISTENT	EXCELLENCE	INCREDIBLE
BASICALLY	CONTINUOUS	EXHAUST	INDEPENDENCE

INDICTED	OCCURRENCE	PRIVILEGE	SHINING
INDISPENSABLE	OFFICIAL	PROBABLY	SIMILAR
INEVITABLE	OPPONENT	PROCEED	SINCERELY
INSURANCE	OPPORTUNITY	PROFESSION	SKIING
INTELLECTUAL	ORDINARILY	PROFESSOR	SOPHOMORE
INTELLIGENCE	ORIGIN	PROMINENT	SPECIFICALLY
INTERESTING	PANICKY	PRONUNCIATION	SPECIMEN
INTERFERENCE	PARALLEL	PROPAGANDA	SPONTANEOUS
INTERRUPT	PARALYSIS	PSYCHOLOGY	STRENGTH
IRRELEVANT	PARALYZE	PUBLICLY	SUBTLE
IRRESISTIBLE	PARTICULAR	QUARANTINE	SUCCEED
JEALOUSY	PARTICULARLY	QUESTIONNAIRE	SUCCESSION
KNOWLEDGE	PASTIME	REALISTICALLY	SUSCEPTIBLE
LABORATORY	PECULIAR	RECEDE	SUSPICIOUS
LEGITIMATE	PERMISSIBLE	RECEIPT	TECHNIQUE
LENGTH	PERSEVERANCE	RECEIVE	TEMPERAMENTAL
LIAISON	PERSISTENCE	RECOMMEND	TEMPERATURE
LICENSE	PERSONNEL	REFERENCE	THEREFORE
LIEUTENANT	PERSPIRATION	REFERRING	TILL
MAINTENANCE	PICNICKING	RELEVANT	TOMORROW
MANAGEABLE	PILGRIMAGE	REMEMBRANCE	TRANSFERRING
MANEUVER	PLAYWRIGHT	REPETITION	TWELFTH
MANUFACTURE	PLEASANT	REPRESENTATIVE	TYRANNY
MATHEMATICS	POSSESSION	RESERVOIR	UNANIMOUS
MILLENNIUM	POSSIBILITY	RESISTANCE	UNDOUBTEDLY
MILLIONAIRE	POTATO	RHYME	UNNECESSARY
MINIATURE	PRACTICALLY	RHYTHM	UNTIL
MISCHIEVOUS	PRECEDE	RIDICULOUS	VACUUM
MISSPELL	PRECEDENCE	ROOMMATE	VILLAIN
MORTGAGE	PREFERENCE	SACRIFICE	VISIBLE
NARRATIVE	PREFERRED	SACRILEGIOUS	WHETHER
NAUSEOUS	PREJUDICE	SALARY	WHOLLY
NECESSARY	PREPARATION	SAVVY	YACHT
NOTICEABLE	PRESCRIPTION	SECRETARY	
NUISANCE	PREVALENT	SEIZE	
OBEDIENCE	PRIMITIVE	SENTENCE	
OBSTACLE	PRINCIPAL	SEPARATE	
OCCURRED	PRINCIPLE	SERGEANT	

USE THIS LETTER WHEN A BREAKUP REQUIRES WRITTEN NOTIFICATION.

INSTRUCTIONS: CUT LETTER ALONG DOTTED LINES. GIVE TO YOUR SOON-TO-BE EX, OR INSERT IN AN ENVELOPE (SEE PAGE 65), AFFIX A STAMP (NOT INCLUDED), AND SEND.

Dear _____,

I know we've been together for a while now, but I am writing to tell you that I can't see you anymore.

Here's why: (Check any/all that apply)

[ ] I met someone else

[ ] You're cheating on me

[ ] I am not attracted to you

[ ] I am only dating you for your money

[ ] I am only dating you for your friends

[ ] I am in love with one of your friends

       (enter friend's name here:_____)

[ ] I hate your friends

[ ] You drink too much

[ ] You are too young/old

[ ] I don't like your new haircut

[ ] I never liked your haircut

[ ] You have a strange odor

[ ] I don't like the way you dress

[ ] You aren't my type

[ ] You have emotional problems

[ ] You are immature

[ ] I am immature

[ ] I am not ready for a relationship

[ ] You are not ready for a relationship

[ ] My parents don't approve

[ ] I am not over my ex

[ ] I am married

[ ] You are married

[ ] You are too clingy

[ ] I am moving to another country

[ ] I want someone better

[ ] Other: _____

Sorry about this. Please (check one) [ ] DO [ ] DON'T call or e-mail me.

Sincerely,

USE THIS LETTER WHEN YOU NEED MONEY. SEND IT TO YOUR MOTHER, FATHER, BROTHER, GRANDMA, GRANDPA, AUNT, UNCLE, FRIEND—WHOEVER MIGHT BE ABLE TO HELP.

INSTRUCTIONS: CUT OUT AT DOTTED LINES. GIVE TO YOUR BENEFACTOR, OR INSERT IN AN ENVELOPE (SEE PAGE 65), AFFIX A STAMP (NOT INCLUDED), AND SEND.

Dear _____,

How are you? I know I rarely write you, but I could use your help. Unfortunately, my financial situation is not as flourishing as it once was. It's not my fault, really; if it weren't for the (Check any/all that apply)

[ ] Tornado/hurricane damages

[ ] Gambling debts

[ ] Credit card charges

[ ] Thieves

[ ] Cost of college

[ ] Cost of children

[ ] Shopping

[ ] Exorbitant independent film investment

[ ] Health insurance costs

[ ] Obsessive-compulsive buying habits

[ ] Lack of a job

[ ] Other: _____

I wouldn't have to ask you for anything. However, the above event(s) have wiped me out. Can you please send $_____. I promise, I will try to pay you back:

(Check any that apply)

[ ] within a month

[ ] within a year

[ ] within five years

[ ] eventually

Thanks so much!

Sincerely,

USE THIS LETTER TO MAKE A PROMISE TO PAY SOMEONE BACK.

INSTRUCTIONS: CUT OUT AT DOTTED LINES. FILL IN THE BLANKS AS INDICATED. GIVE TO YOUR BENEFACTOR, OR INSERT IN AN ENVELOPE (SEE PAGE 65), AFFIX A STAMP (NOT INCLUDED), AND SEND.

PROMISSORY NOTE

DATE:

DEAR _____,

LET THIS LETTER SERVE AS WRITTEN CONFIRMATION

OF MY INTENT TO PAY YOU BACK THE _____
(AMOUNT)

THAT YOU LENT ME ON _____. IF IT WEREN'T
(DATE)

FOR YOUR HELP, I'D NEVER HAVE BEEN ABLE TO

_____

_____.

THANK YOU SO MUCH FOR LENDING ME THE MONEY.
I OWE YOU!

SINCERELY,

GIVE THIS TO YOUR BENEFACTOR AFTER HE OR SHE RESPONDS TO YOUR REQUEST FOR MONEY (SEE PAGE 83).

USE THIS NOTE TO THANK SOMEONE FOR A GIFT.

INSTRUCTIONS: CUT OUT AT DOTTED LINES, FILL IN THE BLANKS, AND SIGN. INSERT IN AN ENVELOPE (SEE PAGE 65), AFFIX A STAMP (NOT INCLUDED), AND SEND.

DEAR _____,

I JUST WANTED TO SEND A LITTLE NOTE
TO THANK YOU FOR YOUR FABULOUS GIFT.
IT WAS SO THOUGHTFUL.
ACTUALLY, I WAS GOING TO GET THE SAME THING
FOR MYSELF JUST RECENTLY—
NOW I DON'T HAVE TO!
HOW DO YOU KNOW ME SO WELL? I LOVE IT!

THANK YOU SO MUCH!

FOLD ▶

Thank You

USE THIS LETTER WHEN YOU ARE UNSATISFIED WITH A STORE, RESTAURANT, OR PUBLIC ESTABLISHMENT.

INSTRUCTIONS: CUT OUT AT DOTTED LINES, SIGN, AND ADDRESS AT TOP. INCLUDE RECEIPT FOR PROOF OF TRANSACTION. INSERT IN AN ENVELOPE (SEE PAGE 65), AFFIX A STAMP (NOT INCLUDED), AND SEND.

_____

_____

_____

_____

[ADDRESS]

DATE_____

To Whom It May Concern,

I am writing this letter in reference to my recent visit to your establishment.

Normally, I'm a very easygoing person and not one to send a letter like this, but the quality of service I received was highly unacceptable. Consequently, I would very much like to be reimbursed for the money I spent while patronizing your business. A customer should not have to pay for service that is so far below reasonable expectations.

Please find my receipt attached. You can send reimbursement to the above address. I thought it best you know the problems inherent in your establishment so that you can deal with them.

Thank you very much.

Sincerely,

ATTACH RECEIPT

USE THIS LETTER WHEN APPLYING FOR EMPLOYMENT.

INSTRUCTIONS: CUT OUT LETTER ALONG DOTTED LINES. INSERT IN AN ENVELOPE (SEE PAGE 65), AFFIX A STAMP (NOT INCLUDED), AND SEND.

Name: _____

Address: _____

_____

Phone Number: _____

E-mail address: _____

Date: _____

To Whom It May Concern:

Subject: Available Position at Your Company

I am writing to you in regard to the available position at your company.

As you can see from my résumé, I have several years of relevant experience that would translate well in an environment such as the one you offer. I've got the skills and professional know-how to be a valuable addition to your team.

I would be happy to further discuss specific elements of my background and qualifications. In addition, I can provide professional as well as personal references upon request. Feel free to contact me at the above number or e-mail address.

Sincerely,

Enclosure: Résumé

USE THIS APPLICATION TO SUBMIT TO POTENTIAL EMPLOYERS.

INSTRUCTIONS: CUT OUT ALONG DOTTED LINES. FILL IN APPLICATION USING BLUE OR BLACK INK. INSERT IN AN ENVELOPE (SEE PAGE 65), AFFIX A STAMP (NOT INCLUDED), AND SEND.

EMPLOYMENT APPLICATION

NAME: _____
(LAST, FIRST, MIDDLE)

TELEPHONE NUMBER: _____

ADDRESS: _____

_____

E-MAIL ADDRESS: _____

ARE YOU APPLYING FOR (CHECK ONE):
☐ FULL TIME ☐ PART TIME ☐ TEMPORARY

WHAT SHIFTS WILL YOU WORK? (CHECK ONE)
☐ DAYS ☐ EVENINGS ☐ NIGHTS

MAY WE CONTACT YOUR PRESENT EMPLOYER?
☐ YES ☐ NO

EMPLOYMENT HISTORY: (BEGIN WITH MOST RECENT)

DATES: _____

COMPANY NAME: _____

ADDRESS: _____

TITLE AND DUTIES: _____

REASON FOR LEAVING: _____

SUPERVISOR'S NAME: _____

PHONE: _____

DATES: _____

COMPANY NAME: _____

ADDRESS: _____

TITLE AND DUTIES: _____

REASON FOR LEAVING: _____

SUPERVISOR'S NAME: _____

PHONE: _____

DATES: _____

COMPANY NAME: _____

ADDRESS: _____

TITLE AND DUTIES: _____

REASON FOR LEAVING: _____

SUPERVISOR'S NAME: _____

PHONE: _____

DATES: _____

COMPANY NAME: _____

ADDRESS: _____

TITLE AND DUTIES: _____

REASON FOR LEAVING: _____

SUPERVISOR'S NAME: _____

PHONE: _____

EDUCATION: _____

SCHOOL: _____

SPECIALIZED COURSES AND TRAINING: _____

_____

_____

OTHER SKILLS:

_____

REFERENCES:

LIST NAMES, ADDRESSES, AND PHONE NUMBERS OF THREE PEOPLE NOT
RELATED TO YOU:

_____

_____

_____

USE THIS LETTER WHEN YOU WANT TO QUIT YOUR JOB.

INSTRUCTIONS: CUT OUT ALONG DOTTED LINES AND SEND IN AN ENVELOPE (SEE PAGE 65), OR HAND DELIVER TO YOUR SUPERIOR.

Date:_____

To:_____

Please accept this letter as my official two weeks' notice of resignation from the company. While I have thoroughly enjoyed my time here, I feel that it's time to move forward with my career and explore new endeavors.

I would like you to know that this decision has nothing to do with the excellent opportunities you have provided me here. On the contrary, my experience with the company has enabled me to further my skills and focus on my goals, and I genuinely appreciate all your support.

Please let me know if there's anything I can do to ensure a smooth transition. It's been a pleasure working with you.

Thanks again.

Sincerely,

USE THIS CERTIFICATE FOR A QUICK AND EASY DECLARATION OF LOVE. (NOTE: THIS IS NOT A LEGAL DOCUMENT.)

INSTRUCTIONS: SIGN, AND HAVE YOUR PARTNER SIGN, IN SPACES PROVIDED. DETACH ALONG DOTTED LINES AND DISPLAY AS A MARK OF YOUR COMMITMENT.

CERTIFICATE OF MARRIAGE

THIS IS TO CERTIFY THAT ON THE _____ DAY OF _____

IN THE YEAR _____

_____ AND _____

WERE UNITED IN MARRIAGE AT _____

IN THE PRESENCE OF THE UNDERSIGNED.

OFFICIATING _____

WITNESSES _____

USE THIS CERTIFICATE

WHEN YOU'RE READY TO BREAK UP, SEE PAGE 81.

CERTIFICATE · USE THIS · CERTIFICATE

USE THIS CERTIFICATE TO PROCLAIM EXCELLENCE.

INSTRUCTIONS: CUT OUT ALONG DOTTED LINES, SIGN, AND DISPLAY PROMINENTLY.

AWARD CERTIFICATE

PROUDLY PRESENTED TO

IN RECOGNITION OF MERITORIOUS SERVICE

RENDERED IN

ON THE _____ DAY OF _____

IN THE YEAR _____ .

OFFICIAL SIGNATURE

USE THIS CERTIFICATE

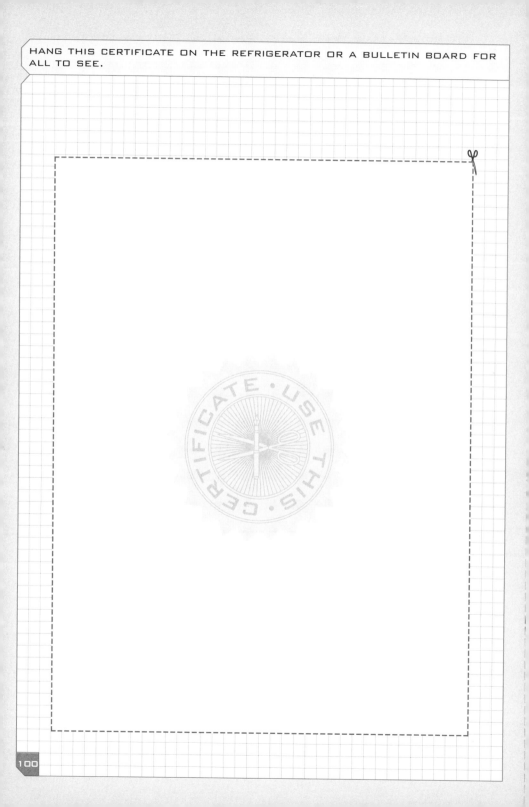

USE THIS CHART TO TEST YOUR VISION.

INSTRUCTIONS: SEE REVERSE SIDE OF THIS PAGE FOR DETAILED INSTRUCTIONS.

E

60

B C

50

P T E O

40

B Z F E D

30

O F C L T B

20

T E P O L F D Z

15

L P C T Z D B F E O

10

Z O E C F L D P B T

7

INSTRUCTIONS: STAND 10 FEET AWAY FROM THE EYE CHART. COVER ONE EYE AND READ EACH LINE OF THE EYE CHART UNTIL THE LETTERS ARE TOO SMALL FOR YOU TO SEE. YOUR VISION ACUITY IS A FRACTION: THE TOP OF THE FRACTION IS 10 (THE DISTANCE IN FEET YOU WERE FROM THE CHART); THE BOTTOM OF THE FRACTION IS THE LINE NUMBER CORRESPONDING TO THE SMALLEST LINE YOU CAN READ. FOR EXAMPLE, IF THE SMALLEST LINE YOU CAN READ IS THE LINE MARKED 20, YOU HAVE A VISUAL ACUITY OF 10/20.

USE THIS GUIDE WHEN YOU'RE SICK AND WANT TO HELP SPEED YOUR RECOVERY.

INSTRUCTIONS: LOOK UP YOUR SYMPTOMS AND FIND THE CORRELATING AILMENT. TREAT AS INDICATED.

COMMON AILMENTS AND THEIR REMEDIES

FOOD ALLERGIES
SYMPTOMS: RASH OR HIVES, NAUSEA, STOMACH PAIN, DIARRHEA, ITCHY SKIN, SHORTNESS OF BREATH, CHEST PAIN, SWELLING OF AIRWAVES TO LUNGS.
WHAT ARE THEY? AN ALLERGIC REACTION CREATED BY THE BODY IN RESPONSE TO A FOOD (USUALLY A PROTEIN). SHELLFISH, PEANUTS, FISH, AND EGGS ARE THE MOST COMMON ADULT ALLERGIES; SOY PRODUCTS, FISH, AND PEANUTS ARE THE MOST COMMON ALLERGIES IN CHILDREN.
HOW IS IT TRANSMITTED? NOT CONTAGIOUS.
REMEDY: AVOID OR REDUCE PROBLEM FOODS. IN THE EVENT OF A SEVERE REACTION, SEEK PROFESSIONAL HELP IMMEDIATELY.

BRONCHITIS
SYMPTOMS: COUGHING (WITH MUCUS), WHEEZING.
WHAT IS IT? A VIRUS (OCCASIONALLY CAUSED BY BACTERIA, BUT NOT COMMONLY).
HOW IS IT TRANSMITTED? THROUGH BREATHING AIR CONTAMINATED WITH THE VIRUS (AFTER AN INFECTED PERSON COUGHS OR SNEEZES). CONTAGIOUS.
REMEDY: MOST CASES WILL GO AWAY ON THEIR OWN; INHALANT SPRAYS MAY ALLEVIATE THE COUGHING. A DOCTOR CAN PRESCRIBE MEDICINE TO HELP OPEN THE BRONCHIAL TUBES AND CLEAR OUT MUCUS.

COLD
SYMPTOMS: FATIGUE, SNEEZING, COUGHING, RUNNY NOSE, LOW-GRADE FEVER, MUSCLE ACHES, SORE THROAT, WATERY EYES, AND HEADACHE.
WHAT IS IT? A VIRUS.
HOW IS IT TRANSMITTED? THROUGH TOUCHING CONTAMINATED SURFACES OR BREATHING CONTAMINATED AIR (SUCH AS AFTER AN INFECTED PERSON SNEEZES), KISSING OR SHARING PERSONAL ITEMS (TOOTHBRUSH, RAZORS, LIPSTICK) WITH INFECTED PERSON. VERY CONTAGIOUS.
REMEDY: THERE IS NO CURE FOR A COLD. IT WILL GO AWAY ON ITS OWN. REST, PLENTY OF FLUIDS, GARGLING WITH SALT WATER, AND TAKING ACETAMINOPHEN, COUGH MEDICINES, AND DECONGESTANTS CAN HELP EASE SYMPTOMS.

1 OF 4

FLU

SYMPTOMS: WEAKNESS, FATIGUE, FEVER, DRY COUGH, RUNNY NOSE, CHILLS, MUSCLE ACHES, HEADACHE, SORE THROAT, AND EYE PAIN.

WHAT IS IT? A VIRUS.

HOW IS IT TRANSMITTED? THROUGH TOUCHING CONTAMINATED SURFACES OR BREATHING CONTAMINATED AIR (SUCH AS AFTER AN INFECTED PERSON SNEEZES), KISSING, OR SHARING PERSONAL ITEMS (TOOTHBRUSH, RAZORS, LIPSTICK) WITH INFECTED PERSON. VERY CONTAGIOUS.

REMEDY: THERE IS NO CURE FOR THE FLU. IT WILL GO AWAY ON ITS OWN. REST, PLENTY OF FLUIDS, GARGLING WITH SALT WATER, AND TAKING ACETAMINOPHEN, COUGH MEDICINES, AND DECONGESTANTS CAN HELP EASE SYMPTOMS.

GASTROENTERITIS (STOMACH FLU)

SYMPTOMS: MUSCLE ACHES, SORE THROAT, NAUSEA OR VOMITING, AND DIARRHEA.

WHAT IS IT? A VIRUS.

HOW IS IT TRANSMITTED? THROUGH TOUCHING CONTAMINATED SURFACES OR BREATHING CONTAMINATED AIR (SUCH AS AFTER AN INFECTED PERSON SNEEZES), KISSING, OR SHARING PERSONAL ITEMS (TOOTHBRUSH, RAZORS, LIPSTICK) WITH INFECTED PERSON. CONTAGIOUS.

TREATMENT: THERE IS NO CURE FOR THE STOMACH FLU; IT WILL GO AWAY ON ITS OWN. REST AND PLENTY OF FLUIDS WILL EASE SYMPTOMS. IF YOU ARE VOMITING, DON'T EAT OR DRINK ANYTHING FOR FOUR HOURS, THEN TAKE SMALL SIPS OF WATER AND WORK UP TO LARGER AMOUNTS. SALTINES OR DRY TOAST MAY ALSO HELP.

HEARTBURN

SYMPTOMS: FEELING OF WARMTH, PRESSURE, OR BURNING IN THE CHEST.

WHAT IS IT? ACID INDIGESTION. HEARTBURN OCCURS WHEN THERE IS ABNORMAL BACKFLOW OF STOMACH ACID INTO THE ESOPHAGUS.

HOW IS IT TRANSMITTED? GENERALLY OCCURS AFTER EATING A LARGE MEAL OR DRINKING A LOT OF ALCOHOL. SOME PEOPLE GET HEARTBURN WHEN THEY BEND OVER OR LIE DOWN. NOT CONTAGIOUS.

REMEDY: AVOID LARGE OR FATTY MEALS, TRY NOT TO EAT BEFORE GOING TO BED, AND DECREASE COFFEE AND ALCOHOL INTAKE. ANTACIDS CAN HELP EASE SYMPTOMS. IF CHEST PAIN PERSISTS OR IS ACCOMPANIED BY OTHER SYMPTOMS (INCLUDING LIGHTHEADEDNESS, SWEATING, AND RAPID PULSE), CALL FOR HELP IMMEDIATELY.

2 OF 4

CONTINUED FROM PAGE 104

MIGRAINE

SYMPTOMS: THROBBING PAIN ON ONE OR BOTH SIDES OF THE HEAD, NAUSEA, AND SENSITIVITY TO NOISE AND LIGHT. OFTEN, PROBLEMS WITH EYESIGHT (BLIND SPOTS, VISION ON JUST ONE SIDE) OCCUR JUST BEFORE A MIGRAINE. MIGRAINES CAN LAST 4 TO 72 HOURS.

WHAT IS IT? DISABLING HEADACHES OFTEN ACCOMPANIED BY NAUSEA.

HOW IS IT TRANSMITTED? GENERALLY THOUGHT TO BE CAUSED BY PROBLEMS WITH THE NERVES AND BLOOD VESSELS IN THE HEAD. NOT CONTAGIOUS.

REMEDY: APPLYING COLD COMPRESSES, RESTING IN A DARK ROOM, AVOIDING STRONG ODORS, MODERATING CAFFEINE INTAKE, OR ADMINISTERING PAIN MEDICATION. PHYSICIANS CAN PRESCRIBE STRONGER MEDICINES FOR SEVERE OR FREQUENT MIGRAINES.

MONONUCLEOSIS

SYMPTOMS: FATIGUE, MILD FEVER, SORE THROAT, HEADACHES, WHITE PATCHES ON THE BACK OF THE THROAT, SWOLLEN GLANDS, AND LACK OF APPETITE.

WHAT IS IT? A VIRAL INFECTION.

HOW IS IT TRANSMITTED? THROUGH CONTACT WITH SALIVA AND MUCUS OF AN INFECTED PERSON. CONTAGIOUS.

TREATMENT: RESTING, TAKING ACETAMINOPHEN, AND GARGLING WITH SALT WATER WILL ALL EASE SYMPTOMS. THE VIRUS WILL USUALLY GO AWAY WITHIN 4 TO 6 WEEKS.

SINUS INFECTION

SYMPTOMS: HEADACHE; PRESSURE IN THE EYES, NOSE, AND CHEEK AREA OR ON ONE SIDE OF THE HEAD; COUGH; FEVER; BAD BREATH; AND NASAL CONGESTION.

WHAT IS IT? AN INFLAMMATION OF THE SINUSES AND NASAL PASSAGES.

HOW IS IT TRANSMITTED? GENERALLY FOLLOWS VIRAL INFECTIONS OF THE UPPER RESPIRATORY TRACT; ALLERGENS MAY TRIGGER SINUS INFECTIONS. NOT CONTAGIOUS.

REMEDY: DRINK PLENTY OF FLUIDS (TO AID IN DRAINAGE). TAKE EXPECTORANTS AND DECONGESTANTS TO HELP THIN THE MUCUS LINING IN RESPIRATORY SYSTEM, COUGH AND PAIN MEDICATIONS TO EASE SYMPTOMS, AND NASAL SPRAYS AND ANTIBIOTICS TO RID THE BODY OF THE OFFENDING BACTERIA.

STREP THROAT

WHAT IS IT? A BACTERIAL INFECTION.

HOW IS IT TRANSMITTED? THROUGH CONTACT WITH MUCUS OR SALIVA OF AN INFECTED PERSON. VERY CONTAGIOUS.

SYMPTOMS: WHITE PATCHES ON TONSILS, HEADACHE, SORE THROAT, SWOLLEN NECK GLANDS, AND FEVER.

TREATMENT: ANTIBIOTICS (PENICILLIN). ACETAMINOPHEN AND GARGLING WITH SALT WATER CAN HELP EASE SYMPTOMS.

ULCER

WHAT IS IT? AN AREA IN THE DIGESTIVE SYSTEM WHERE TISSUE HAS BEEN DESTROYED BY GASTRIC JUICES AND STOMACH ACID.

HOW IS IT TRANSMITTED? GENERALLY CAUSED BY AN IMBALANCE BETWEEN ACID AND PEPSIN AND THE DIGESTIVE TRACT'S INABILITY TO PROTECT ITSELF FROM THESE HARSH SUBSTANCES. LIFESTYLE FACTORS SUCH AS STRESS MAY INCREASE CHANCES OF THIS IMBALANCE (BUT IT IS NOT ALWAYS A FACTOR). CERTAIN MEDICATIONS CAN ALSO CONTRIBUTE, INCLUDING ASPIRIN AND NONSTEROIDAL ANTI-INFLAMMATORY DRUGS (SUCH AS IBUPROFEN AND NAPROXEN). CAFFEINE AND ALCOHOL CAN ALSO CONTRIBUTE. NOT CONTAGIOUS.

SYMPTOMS: BURNING PAIN IN UPPER MIDDLE PART OF THE ABDOMEN, ABOVE THE BELLY BUTTON. PAIN IS WORSE AT NIGHT AND EARLY MORNING, AND IT MOST OFTEN OCCURS WHEN THE STOMACH IS EMPTY. PAIN IS OFTEN RELIEVED BY TAKING ANTACIDS OR EATING A MEAL.

REMEDY: AVOID CAFFEINE, ALCOHOL, NICOTINE, AND ASPIRIN OR NSAIDS. ANTACIDS AND NONPRESCRIPTION HISTAMINE (H2) BLOCKERS CAN HELP MILD ULCERS; MORE SEVERE ULCERS REQUIRE MEDICAL CARE.

4 OF 4

USE THIS CHART TO DETERMINE IF YOUR MOLES ARE INDICATIVE OF CANCER.

INSTRUCTIONS: DETACH CHART ALONG DOTTED LINES AND KEEP IN THE BATHROOM OR BEDROOM FOR EASY REFERENCE. YOU SHOULD CHECK YOUR MOLES FREQUENTLY TO TRACK POSSIBLE CHANGES IN COLOR AND SHAPE.

SKIN CANCER CHECK SHEET

USE THE **ABCD** RULE TO HELP YOU REMEMBER WHAT TO LOOK FOR WHEN INSPECTING YOUR MOLES.

ASYMMETRY: WHEN ONE HALF OF THE MOLE DOES NOT MATCH THE OTHER HALF.

BORDER IRREGULARITY: WHEN THE EDGES ARE RAGGED OR BLURRED.

COLOR: WHEN THE COLOR IS NOT THE SAME ALL OVER.

DIAMETER: WHEN THE MOLE IS GREATER THAN ONE QUARTER OF AN INCH (.6 CM) IN SIZE.

A	B	C	D
ASYMMETRY	BORDER	COLOR	DIAMETER

USE THESE TIPS TO HELP PREVENT SKIN CANCER. REMEMBER:
APPROXIMATELY ONE OUT OF SIX PEOPLE WILL DEVELOP SKIN CANCER.
PREVENTION IS KEY!

SKIN CANCER PREVENTION TIPS

TRY TO STAY OUT OF THE SUN DURING PEAK HOURS, BETWEEN 11
A.M. AND 3 P.M., WHEN THE RAYS ARE MOST HARMFUL.

ALWAYS WEAR A BROAD-SPECTRUM SUNSCREEN WITH AN SPF OF
15 OR HIGHER, EVEN WHILE INSIDE OR DRIVING. ULTRAVIOLET RAYS
CAN GO THROUGH CAR AND RESIDENTIAL WINDOWS. UNDERSTAND
SPF: THE SPF RATING REFERS TO THE AMOUNT OF TIME YOU CAN BE
IN THE SUN BEFORE YOU BURN, COMPARED TO USING NO SUN-
SCREEN. A SUNSCREEN WITH AN SPF OF 15 ALLOWS YOU TO
REMAIN IN THE SUN WITHOUT BURNING 15 TIMES LONGER THAN IF
YOU DIDN'T APPLY SUNSCREEN.

APPLY SUNSCREEN 30 TO 45 MINUTES BEFORE SUN EXPOSURE TO
ALLOW PRODUCT TO PENETRATE THE SKIN.

WEAR SUNSCREEN WHILE SWIMMING, SINCE UV RAYS CAN
PENETRATE AT LEAST THREE FEET (90 CM) INTO THE WATER.

WEAR A WIDE-BRIMMED HAT AND UV-BLOCKING GLASSES TO
PROTECT YOUR EARS, FACE, AND EYES.

NOTE THAT SUN RAYS REFLECT OFF SNOW, SAND, AND WATER.
YOU ARE NOT PROTECTED IF UNDER A BEACH UMBRELLA OR WHILE
SKIING.

WEAR TIGHTLY-WOVEN FABRICS THAT THE SUN CANNOT PENETRATE.

DON'T GET BURNED. EVEN ONE BLISTERING SUNBURN INCREASES
YOUR RISK OF MELANOMA.

CHECK YOUR SKIN EVERY MONTH FOR NEW OR UNUSUAL GROWTHS
(SEE OTHER SIDE) AND SEE A DERMATOLOGIST IMMEDIATELY IF ANY-
THING LOOKS SUSPICIOUS.

USE THIS CHART TO DETERMINE A HEALTHY WEIGHT FOR YOUR HEIGHT.

INSTRUCTIONS: CUT OUT CHART ALONG DOTTED LINES AND POST ON THE REFRIGERATOR FOR EASY REFERENCE. TO FIND IF YOU ARE AT A HEALTHY WEIGHT, LINE UP YOUR HEIGHT (LEFT SIDE) WITH YOUR WEIGHT (BOTTOM).

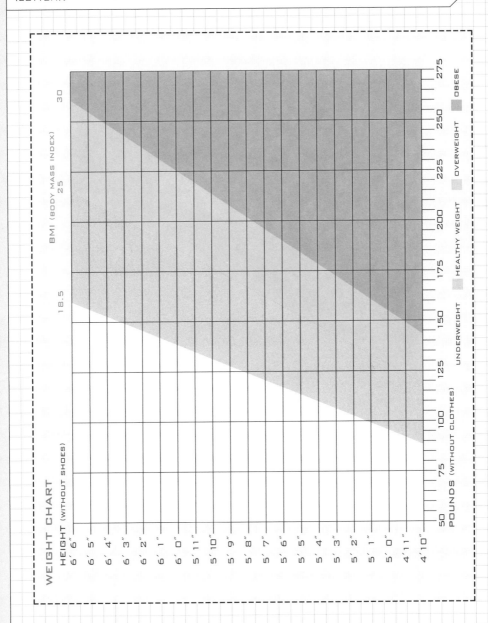

WEIGHT CHART

USE THIS CHART TO DETERMINE HOW MANY CALORIES YOU'RE BURNING DOING VARIOUS ACTIVITIES. DAILY EXERCISE WILL HELP YOU MAINTAIN A HEALTHY WEIGHT (SEE OTHER SIDE).

INSTRUCTIONS: CUT ALONG DOTTED LINES AND KEEP WITH YOU AT THE GYM, AT THE PARK, OR OTHER PLACE WHERE YOU MAY WANT TO SEE YOUR CALORIE-BURNING CAPACITY.

CALORIE-BURNING CHART

ACTIVITY (PER 1 HOUR)	APPROXIMATE CALORIES BURNED BY WEIGHT CLASS		
	130 LBS	155 LBS	190 LBS
AEROBICS	350	425	525
ARCHERY	200	250	300
AUTOMOBILE REPAIR	175	225	250
BACKPACKING	425	500	600
BASKETBALL	350	425	525
BICYCLING, MODERATE EFFORT	475	575	700
MOUNTAIN BIKING	500	600	725
BICYCLING, STATIONARY	425	500	600
BILLIARDS	150	175	225
BOWLING	175	225	220
BOXING	700	850	1050
CALISTHENICS (SIT-UPS, PUSH-UPS)	275	325	375
CANOEING, ROWING	425	500	600
CARPENTRY, GENERAL	200	250	300
CHILD CARE	175	225	250
CLEANING	200	250	300
CONSTRUCTION	325	400	475
DANCING	275	325	375
FENCING	350	425	525
FOOTBALL	525	625	775
FOOTBALL, TOUCH, FLAG	475	550	700
FRISBEE PLAYING, GENERAL	175	225	250
GARDENING	300	350	425
GOLF	250	275	350
GYMNASTICS	250	275	350
HIKING	350	425	525
HORSEBACK RIDING	250	275	350
JOGGING	425	500	600
MOVING FURNITURE	350	425	525
PUSHING STROLLER	150	175	225
RAKING LAWN	250	275	350
ROCK CLIMBING (ASCENDING ROCK)	650	775	950
ROPE JUMPING	600	700	875
ROWING, STATIONARY	425	500	600
RUNNING	475	575	700
SAILING	175	225	250
SKATING, ICE	400	500	600
SKIING, SNOW	400	500	600
SKIING, WATER	350	425	525
SNORKELING	300	350	425
SOCCER	425	500	600
SQUASH	700	850	1050
SURFING, BODY OR BOARD	175	225	250
SWIMMING LAPS, FREESTYLE	475	550	700
TENNIS, GENERAL	425	500	600
VOLLEYBALL, BEACH	472	575	700
VOLLEYBALL, IN GYMNASIUM	250	275	350
WALKING, MODERATE PACE	200	250	300
WEIGHT LIFTING	175	225	250
WHITEWATER RAFTING	295	350	425
YOGA, HATHA	250	275	350

USE THIS CHART TO IDENTIFY VARIOUS PARTS OF THE HUMAN MUSCULAR SYSTEM. THE HUMAN BODY IS MADE UP OF MORE THAN 650 DIFFERENT MUSCLES.

INSTRUCTIONS: CUT OUT ALONG DOTTED LINES. FOR INSTRUCTIONS ON HOW TO USE ACUPRESSURE, SEE PAGE 115.

MUSCULAR SYSTEM

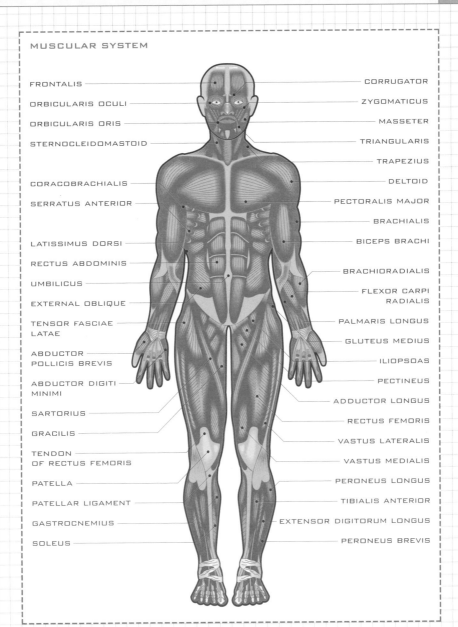

FRONTALIS

ORBICULARIS OCULI

ORBICULARIS ORIS

STERNOCLEIDOMASTOID

CORACOBRACHIALIS

SERRATUS ANTERIOR

LATISSIMUS DORSI

RECTUS ABDOMINIS

UMBILICUS

EXTERNAL OBLIQUE

TENSOR FASCIAE LATAE

ABDUCTOR POLLICIS BREVIS

ABDUCTOR DIGITI MINIMI

SARTORIUS

GRACILIS

TENDON OF RECTUS FEMORIS

PATELLA

PATELLAR LIGAMENT

GASTROCNEMIUS

SOLEUS

CORRUGATOR

ZYGOMATICUS

MASSETER

TRIANGULARIS

TRAPEZIUS

DELTOID

PECTORALIS MAJOR

BRACHIALIS

BICEPS BRACHI

BRACHIORADIALIS

FLEXOR CARPI RADIALIS

PALMARIS LONGUS

GLUTEUS MEDIUS

ILIOPSOAS

PECTINEUS

ADDUCTOR LONGUS

RECTUS FEMORIS

VASTUS LATERALIS

VASTUS MEDIALIS

PERONEUS LONGUS

TIBIALIS ANTERIOR

EXTENSOR DIGITORUM LONGUS

PERONEUS BREVIS

SKELETAL SYSTEM

SKULL

ORBITAL CAVITY

MAXILLA — MANDIBLE

VERTEBRAE

CLAVICLE

SCAPULA

STERNUM

RIB

HUMERUS

COSTAL CARTILAGE

RADIUS — ILIUM

ULNA — SACRUM

CARPALS — COCCYX

METACARPALS — PUBIS

PHALANGES

FEMUR

PATELLA

FIBULA

TIBIA

TARSAL

METATARSAL

PHALANGE

USE THIS CHART TO ALLEVIATE MINOR ACHES AND PAINS BY ACTIVATING PRESSURE POINTS IN THE FEET.

INSTRUCTIONS: CUT OUT CARD ALONG DOTTED LINES. APPLY MODERATE PRESSURE WITH YOUR FINGERTIPS TO SPECIFIC AREAS AS NECESSARY.

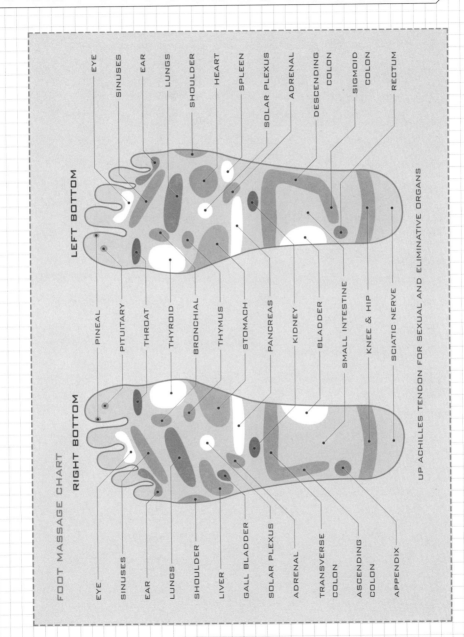

FOOT MASSAGE CHART

LEFT BOTTOM

RIGHT BOTTOM

EYE
SINUSES
EAR
LUNGS
SHOULDER
HEART
SPLEEN
SOLAR PLEXUS
ADRENAL
DESCENDING COLON
SIGMOID COLON
RECTUM

PINEAL
PITUITARY
THROAT
THYROID
BRONCHIAL
THYMUS
STOMACH
PANCREAS
KIDNEY
BLADDER
SMALL INTESTINE
KNEE & HIP
SCIATIC NERVE

EYE
SINUSES
EAR
LUNGS
SHOULDER
LIVER
GALL BLADDER
SOLAR PLEXUS
ADRENAL
TRANSVERSE COLON
ASCENDING COLON
APPENDIX

UP ACHILLES TENDON FOR SEXUAL AND ELIMINATIVE ORGANS

USE THIS CHART TO FIND SPECIFIC PRESSURE POINTS ON YOUR HANDS THAT CAN BE AS THERAPEUTIC AS A FOOT MASSAGE.

INSTRUCTIONS: CUT OUT CHART AND KEEP WITH YOU FOR TIMES WHEN YOU NEED TO KEEP YOUR SHOES AND SOCKS ON.

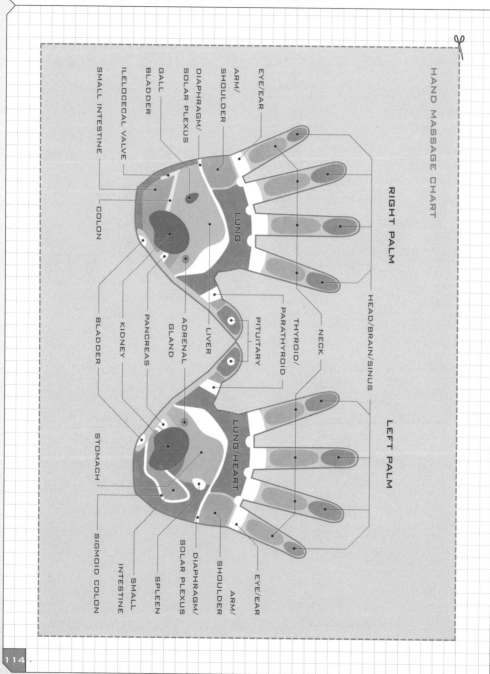

HAND MASSAGE CHART

RIGHT PALM

LEFT PALM

EYE/EAR

ARM/ SHOULDER

DIAPHRAGM/ SOLAR PLEXUS

GALL BLADDER

ILEOCECAL VALVE

SMALL INTESTINE

COLON

LUNG

HEAD/BRAIN/SINUS

NECK

THYROID/ PARATHYROID

PITUITARY

LIVER

ADRENAL GLAND

PANCREAS

KIDNEY

BLADDER

STOMACH

LUNG/HEART

EYE/EAR

ARM/ SHOULDER

DIAPHRAGM/ SOLAR PLEXUS

SPLEEN

SMALL INTESTINE

SIGMOID COLON

USE THIS CHART TO ALLEVIATE MINOR ACHES AND PAINS BY ACTIVATING THE PRESSURE POINTS.

INSTRUCTIONS: CUT OUT CARD ALONG DOTTED LINES. APPLY MODERATE PRESSURE WITH YOUR FINGERTIPS TO SPECIFIC AREAS AS NECESSARY.

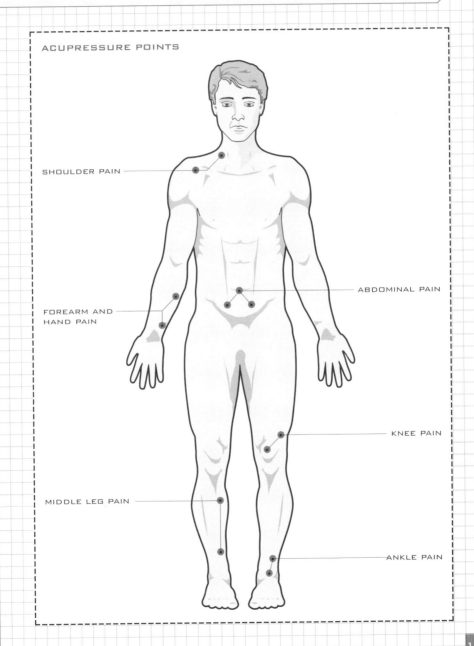

ACUPRESSURE POINTS

SHOULDER PAIN

FOREARM AND HAND PAIN

ABDOMINAL PAIN

KNEE PAIN

MIDDLE LEG PAIN

ANKLE PAIN

ACUPRESSURE POINTS

NECK PAIN

SHOULDER PAIN

LOWER BACK PAIN

THIGH PAIN

USE THESE POSITIONS TO HELP STRENGTHEN YOUR MUSCLES AND EASE TENSION IN YOUR BODY.

INSTRUCTIONS: CUT OUT ALONG DOTTED LINES AND KEEP HANDY FOR WHEN YOU NEED SOME RECENTERING.

YOGA POSITIONS

CHILD'S POSE
HOW TO DO IT: SIT BACK ON YOUR HEELS WITH THE TOPS OF YOUR FEET ON THE FLOOR. BRING YOUR CHEST TO THE GROUND AND PLACE YOUR ARMS AT YOUR SIDES. PLACE YOUR HEAD WHEREVER COMFORTABLE (TO THE SIDE OR FACING DOWN). HOLD FOR AS LONG AS YOU LIKE.

WHAT IT DOES: RELAXES THE BODY AND MIND, EASES TENSION.

WARRIOR POSE
HOW TO DO IT: STAND WITH YOUR FEET TOGETHER AND YOUR ELBOWS BENT WITH YOUR PALMS TOGETHER. STEP BACK WITH YOUR LEFT FOOT AS FAR AS YOU CAN WITHOUT AFFECTING YOUR BALANCE. BEND YOUR RIGHT LEG INTO A LUNGE AND HOLD. BRING ARMS OUT IN FRONT OF YOU, WITH YOUR PALMS STILL PRESSED TOGETHER, THEN EXTEND YOUR ARMS BACK OVERHEAD, ARCHING YOUR BACK AND LOOKING UP, IF YOU CAN. REPEAT ON THE OPPOSITE SIDE.

WHAT IT DOES: PROMOTES BALANCE, STRETCHES THE SPINE, EASES BACK AND SHOULDER TENSION.

YOGA POSITIONS

BRIDGE

HOW TO DO IT: LIE ON YOUR BACK WITH YOUR FEET ON THE GROUND AND YOUR LEGS BENT. EXHALE SLOWLY AS YOU RAISE YOUR HIPS OFF THE GROUND. CLASP YOUR HANDS UNDER YOUR BACK. HOLD FOR SEVERAL MINUTES. SLOWLY LOWER DOWN. REPEAT THREE OR FOUR TIMES.

WHAT IT DOES: STRENGTHENS THE LOWER BACK, BUTT, AND THIGHS.

FROG

HOW TO DO IT: STAND UPRIGHT WITH PALMS PRESSED TOGETHER. YOUR FEET SHOULD BE ABOUT SHOULDER-WIDTH APART AND POINTING OUT AT ABOUT A 45 DEGREE ANGLE. SLOWLY SQUAT DOWN, KEEPING PALMS TOGETHER, ENDING WITH KNEES POINTED OUT IN A CROUCHING FROG POSE. HOLD FOR A FEW MINUTES, THEN EXHALE AND STAND. REPEAT FOUR TO FIVE TIMES.

WHAT IT DOES: STRENGTHENS THE THIGH MUSCLES.

USE THIS CARD TO DETERMINE AN APPROPRIATE TIP.

INSTRUCTIONS: CUT ALONG DOTTED LINES. KEEP CARD IN YOUR WALLET FOR EASY REFERENCE.

TIP TABLE 15% TO 20%

CHECK	15%	20%	CHECK	15%	20%
$1.00	$0.15	$0.20	$26.00	$3.90	$5.20
2.00	0.30	0.40	27.00	4.05	5.40
3.00	0.30	0.40	28.00	4.20	5.60
4.00	0.60	0.80	29.00	4.35	5.80
5.00	0.75	1.00	30.00	4.50	6.00
6.00	0.90	1.20	31.00	4.65	6.20
7.00	1.05	1.40	32.00	4.80	6.40
8.00	1.20	1.60	33.00	4.95	6.60
9.00	1.35	1.80	34.00	5.10	6.80
10.00	1.50	2.00	35.00	5.25	7.00
11.00	1.65	2.20	36.00	5.40	7.20
12.00	1.80	2.40	37.00	5.55	7.40
13.00	1.95	2.60	38.00	5.70	7.60
14.00	2.10	2.80	39.00	5.85	7.80
15.00	2.25	3.00	40.00	6.00	8.00
16.00	2.40	3.20	41.00	6.15	8.20
17.00	2.55	3.40	42.00	6.30	8.40
18.00	2.70	3.60	43.00	6.45	8.60
19.00	2.85	3.80	44.00	6.60	8.80
20.00	3.00	4.00	45.00	6.75	9.00
21.00	3.15	4.20	46.00	6.90	9.20
22.00	3.30	4.40	47.00	7.05	9.40
23.00	3.45	4.60	48.00	7.20	9.60
24.00	3.60	4.80	49.00	7.35	9.80
25.00	3.75	5.00	50.00	7.50	10.00

IN MOST PLACES IN THE UNITED STATES, 15–20% TIP IS STANDARD. BE AWARE THAT IN SOME COUNTRIES, TIPPING IS NOT CUSTOMARY OR NECESSARY.

TIP TABLE 15% TO 20%

CHECK	15%	20%	CHECK	15%	20%
$51.00	$7.65	$10.20	$76.00	$11.40	$15.20
52.00	7.80	10.40	77.00	11.55	15.40
53.00	7.95	10.60	78.00	11.70	15.60
54.00	8.10	10.80	79.00	11.85	15.80
55.00	8.25	11.00	80.00	12.00	15.00
56.00	8.40	11.20	81.00	12.15	16.20
57.00	8.55	11.40	82.00	12.30	16.40
58.00	8.70	11.60	83.00	12.45	16.60
59.00	8.85	11.80	84.00	12.60	16.80
60.00	9.00	11.00	85.00	12.75	17.00
61.00	9.15	12.20	86.00	12.90	17.20
62.00	9.30	12.40	87.00	13.05	17.40
63.00	9.45	12.60	88.00	13.20	17.60
64.00	9.60	12.80	89.00	13.35	17.80
65.00	9.75	13.00	90.00	13.50	18.00
66.00	9.90	13.20	91.00	13.65	18.20
67.00	10.05	13.40	92.00	13.80	18.40
68.00	10.20	13.60	93.00	13.95	18.60
69.00	10.35	13.80	94.00	14.10	18.80
70.00	10.50	14.00	95.00	14.25	19.00
71.00	10.65	14.20	96.00	14.40	19.20
72.00	10.80	14.40	97.00	14.55	19.40
73.00	10.95	14.60	98.00	14.70	19.60
74.00	11.10	14.80	99.00	14.85	19.80
75.00	11.25	15.00	100.00	15.00	20.00

USE THIS GUIDE TO DETERMINE THE APPROXIMATE CALORIE AND FAT CONTENT OF FAST FOODS.

INSTRUCTIONS: DETACH ALONG DOTTED LINES AND KEEP IN YOUR WALLET FOR EASY REFERENCE.

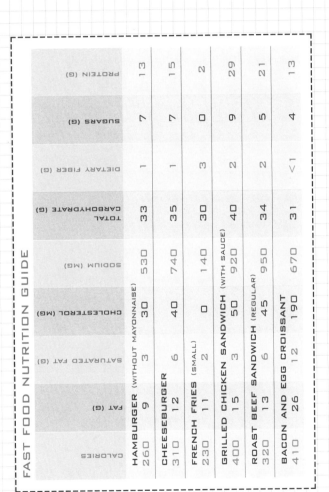

FAST FOOD NUTRITION GUIDE

	CALORIES	FAT (G)	SATURATED FAT (G)	CHOLESTEROL (MG)	SODIUM (MG)	TOTAL CARBOHYDRATE (G)	DIETARY FIBER (G)	SUGARS (G)	PROTEIN (G)
HAMBURGER (WITHOUT MAYONNAISE)	260	9	3	30	530	33	1	7	13
CHEESEBURGER	310	12	6	40	740	35	1	7	15
FRENCH FRIES (SMALL)	230	11	2	0	140	30	3	0	2
GRILLED CHICKEN SANDWICH (WITH SAUCE)	400	15	3	50	920	40	2	9	29
ROAST BEEF SANDWICH (REGULAR)	320	13	6	45	950	34	2	5	21
BACON AND EGG CROISSANT	410	26	12	190	670	31	<1	4	13

FAST FOOD NUTRITION GUIDE

	CALORIES	FAT (G)	SATURATED FAT (G)	CHOLESTEROL (MG)	SODIUM (MG)	TOTAL CARBOHYDRATE (G)	DIETARY FIBER (G)	SUGARS (G)	PROTEIN (G)
CAESAR SALAD WITH CHICKEN (WITH DRESSING)	390	24	6.5	90	1330	14	3	6	30
CHICKEN NUGGETS (6 PIECE)	250	15	3	35	670	15	0	0	15
VANILLA MILKSHAKE (REGULAR)	500	15	11	45	320	75	0	75	12
PIZZA (ONE SLICE CHEESE)	300	11	3.5	20	750	39	2	6	13
DONUT (GLAZED)	200	12	3	5	95	22	<1	10	2
SODA (MEDIUM)	200	0	0	0	15	58	0	58	0

USE THIS CHART TO DETERMINE A "SERVING SIZE" OF A PARTICULAR FOOD GROUP.

INSTRUCTIONS: CUT OUT CARDS, POST ONE IN YOUR KITCHEN FOR EASY REFERENCE, AND TAKE ONE WITH YOU FOR PROPER SERVING SIZES ON THE GO.

SERVING SIZE CHART

RICE AND PASTA
  ONE SERVING IS THE SIZE OF A BASEBALL.

SALAD DRESSING, MAYONNAISE, OR PEANUT
  BUTTER
  ONE SERVING IS THE TIP OF THUMB FROM END
  OF THE NAIL TO THE FIRST JOINT.

CHEESE
  ONE SERVING IS FOUR STACKED DICE OR A
  STANDARD MATCHBOX.

NUTS, PRETZELS, OR RAISINS
  ONE SERVING IS THE AMOUNT YOU CAN HOLD
  IN ONE CUPPED HAND.

SERVING SIZE CHART

RICE AND PASTA
  ONE SERVING IS THE SIZE OF A BASEBALL.

SALAD DRESSING, MAYONNAISE, OR PEANUT
  BUTTER
  ONE SERVING IS THE TIP OF THUMB FROM END
  OF THE NAIL TO THE FIRST JOINT.

CHEESE
  ONE SERVING IS FOUR STACKED DICE OR A
  STANDARD MATCHBOX.

NUTS, PRETZELS, OR RAISINS
  ONE SERVING IS THE AMOUNT YOU CAN HOLD
  IN ONE CUPPED HAND.

✂

MEAT
ONE SERVING IS ABOUT SIZE OF A DECK OF CARDS.

FRUIT
ONE SERVING IS ABOUT THE SIZE OF A SMALL FIST.

POTATOES
ONE SERVING IS THE SIZE OF A COMPUTER MOUSE.

BAGELS
ONE SERVING IS THE SIZE OF A HOCKEY PUCK

PANCAKES
ONE SERVING IS THE SIZE OF A COMPACT DISC

✂

MEAT
ONE SERVING IS ABOUT SIZE OF A DECK OF CARDS.

FRUIT
ONE SERVING IS ABOUT THE SIZE OF A SMALL FIST.

POTATOES
ONE SERVING IS THE SIZE OF A COMPUTER MOUSE.

BAGELS
ONE SERVING IS THE SIZE OF A HOCKEY PUCK

PANCAKES
ONE SERVING IS THE SIZE OF A COMPACT DISC

USE THIS RECIPE TO MAKE CHICKEN SOUP.

INSTRUCTIONS: CUT OUT RECIPE CARD FROM PAGE AND KEEP IN THE KITCHEN FOR EASY REFERENCE.

CHICKEN SOUP RECIPE

INGREDIENTS:
1 WHOLE CHICKEN
1 GALLON (3.8 L) WATER (ENOUGH TO COVER CHICKEN)
1 ONION, CUT IN QUARTERS
3 GARLIC CLOVES
2 TEASPOONS (10 ML) SALT
1 POUND (4.5 KG) NEW POTATOES
4 LARGE CARROTS, DICED
2 STALKS CELERY, DICED

INSTRUCTIONS:
1. COMBINE CHICKEN, WATER, ONION, GARLIC, GINGER, AND SALT IN A LARGE STOCK POT AND BRING TO A BOIL.
2. SIMMER FOR 45 MINUTES, SKIMMING OFF FAT AS NEEDED, UNTIL CHICKEN IS FULLY COOKED.
3. REMOVE THE CHICKEN AND SHRED THE MEAT, DISCARDING BONES, FAT, AND SKIN.
4. STRAIN CHICKEN BROTH, RETURNING BROTH TO THE PAN.
5. ADD POTATOES, CARROTS, CELERY, AND SHREDDED CHICKEN TO THE BROTH, AND BRING TO A BOIL.
6. REDUCE HEAT AND SIMMER FOR 30 MINUTES OR UNTIL POTATOES ARE DONE. SERVE HOT.

SERVES 12

ONE CUP OF CHICKEN SOUP HAS ABOUT 100 CALORIES, 4 GRAMS OF PROTEIN, 19 GRAMS OF CARBOHYDRATES, AND 2 GRAMS OF FAT. FOR MORE CALORIE COUNTS, SEE PAGE 121.

RECIPE · USE · THIS ·

CHICKEN SOUP RECIPE

USE THESE CARDS WHEN YOU WANT TO MIX A TASTY DRINK FOR YOUR NEXT PARTY.

INSTRUCTIONS: CUT CARD ALONG DOTTED LINES. KEEP THE CARD NEAR YOUR HOME BAR.

CLASSIC COCKTAILS

B-52
1 PART GRAND MARNIER
1 PART KAHLUA
1 PART BAILEY'S IRISH CREAM
TO MAKE: SHAKE INGREDIENTS IN EQUAL PARTS WITH ICE. STRAIN INTO TUMBLERS OR SERVE AS SHOOTERS.

BELLINI
1 PART PEACH SCHNAPPS
3 PARTS CHAMPAGNE
TO MAKE: POUR PEACH SCHNAPPS INTO CHAMPAGNE OR COCKTAIL GLASS AND ADD CHAMPAGNE.

BLACK RUSSIAN
2 PARTS VODKA
1 PART KAHLUA
TO MAKE: POUR VODKA INTO A TUMBLER FILLED WITH ICE. ADD KAHLUA AND STIR.
VARIATION: TO MAKE A WHITE RUSSIAN, REDUCE KAHLUA TO $\frac{1}{2}$ PART, AND ADD $\frac{1}{2}$ PART CREAM.

BLOODY MARY
1.25 OZ. (37 ML) VODKA
2.5 OZ. (74 ML) TOMATO JUICE
DASH OF WORCESTERSHIRE SAUCE
DASH OF TABASCO SAUCE
DASH OF SALT AND PEPPER
TO MAKE: POUR ALL INGREDIENTS INTO A TALL GLASS WITH ICE. GARNISH WITH A CELERY STICK.

COSMOPOLITAN
1 PART COINTREAU
1 PART TRIPLE SEC
2 PARTS VODKA
1 PART LIME JUICE
1 PART CRANBERRY JUICE
TO MAKE: FILL A MIXING GLASS HALFWAY WITH ICE. POUR IN ALL INGREDIENTS, SHAKE, AND STRAIN INTO A CHILLED MARTINI GLASS. GARNISH WITH A LIME WEDGE.

FUZZY NAVEL
1 PART PEACH SCHNAPPS
2 PARTS ORANGE JUICE
TO MAKE: POUR PEACH SCHNAPPS INTO A TUMBLER WITH ICE, ADD ORANGE JUICE AND STIR.

IRISH COFFEE

1.5 OZ. (45 ML) IRISH WHISKEY
HOT COFFEE
SUGAR
CREAM
TO MAKE: POUR IRISH WHISKEY INTO A MUG, FILL WITH COFFEE. ADD SUGAR AND CREAM TO TASTE.

LONG ISLAND ICED TEA

1 PART VODKA
1 PART LIGHT RUM
1 PART GIN
1 PART LIGHT TEQUILA
1 PART TRIPLE SEC
COLA
TO MAKE: SHAKE THE LIQUORS TOGETHER WITH ICE AND STRAIN INTO A TALL GLASS. FILL THE GLASS UP WITH COLA. CAN ALSO BE SERVED OVER ICE.

MANHATTAN

2 OZ. (60 ML) WHISKEY (NOT SCOTCH—USE IRISH OR BOURBON)
1 TBSP. (15 ML) SWEET OR DRY VERMOUTH
DASH ANGOSTURA BITTERS
TO MAKE: POUR INGREDIENTS INTO A TUMBLER, STIR, AND GARNISH WITH A CHERRY.

MARGARITA

1 PART TEQUILA
1 PART COINTREAU OR TRIPLE SEC
1 PART SWEET & SOUR MIX OR LIME JUICE
TO MAKE: SHAKE INGREDIENTS WITH ICE AND STRAIN INTO A SALT-RIMMED MARGARITA GLASS OR COCKTAIL GLASS WITH ICE. GARNISH WITH A SLICE OF LIME.

MARTINI

2 OZ. (60 ML) GIN
DASH EXTRA DRY VERMOUTH
TO MAKE: SHAKE OR STIR THE INGREDIENTS WITH ICE AND STRAIN INTO A COCKTAIL GLASS. GARNISH WITH AN OLIVE OR A LEMON RIND.
VARIATION: TO MAKE A VODKA MARTINI, SUBSTITUTE VODKA FOR THE GIN.

WHISKEY SOUR

1.5 OZ. (45 ML) WHISKEY (NOT SCOTCH OR BOURBON)
1 OZ. (30 ML) LEMON JUICE
1 TSP. (5 ML) POWDERED SUGAR
TO MAKE: SHAKE ALL INGREDIENTS WITH ICE AND STRAIN INTO COCKTAIL GLASS. CAN ALSO BE SERVED OVER ICE.

USE THIS SETTING WHEN YOU NEED HELP ORGANIZING YOUR TABLE FOR A PROPER SUPPER.

INSTRUCTIONS: FOLLOW GUIDE BELOW TO SET UTENSILS AND DINING WARE.

TABLE SETTING

RED WINE

WHITE WINE

WATER GOBLET

SOUP SPOON

TEASPOON

DINNER KNIFE

CAKE FORK

DESSERT SPOON

SOUP BOWL

SERVICE OR DINNER PLATE

BREAD & BUTTER PLATE

BUTTER SPREADER

DESSERT FORK

DINNER FORK

NAPKIN

SALAD FORK

DINNER FORK

USE THE PLACESETTING AS AN AID TO IDENTIFYING WHICH BREAD PLATE
OR WATER GLASS IS YOURS WHEN OUT TO A NICE MEAL.

USE THESE STEP-BY-STEP INSTRUCTIONS TO LEARN THE FOLLOWING SIMPLE DANCES.

INSTRUCTIONS: CUT OUT DANCE CARDS ALONG DOTTED LINES AND KEEP WITH YOU FOR EASY REFERENCE.

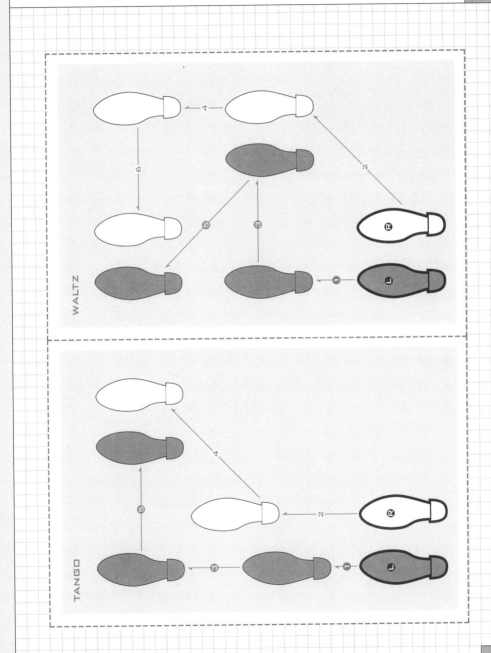

THE STEPS HERE ARE FOR THE PERSON IN THE LEAD; WOMEN SHOULD DO EACH STEP BACKWARD. THE STEPS BEGIN AT THE FOOTPRINTS WITH BOLD OUTLINES.

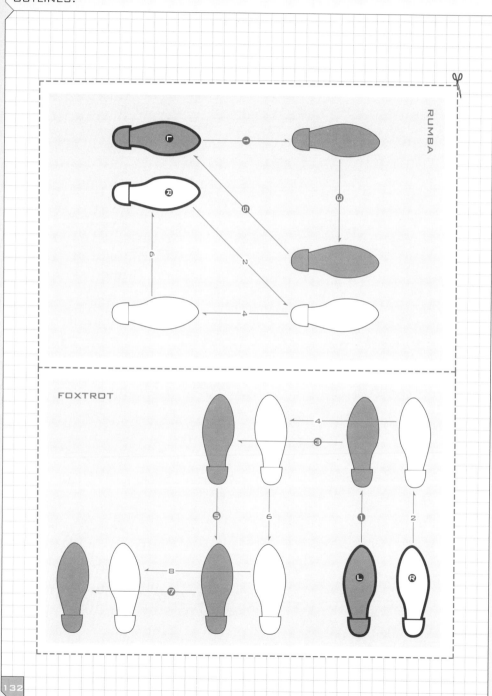

USE THIS DEVICE TO VIEW A SOLAR ECLIPSE WITHOUT DAMAGING YOUR VISION. VIEWING A SOLAR ECLIPSE WITHOUT A PROPER VIEWING DEVICE COULD CAUSE BLINDNESS OR PERMANENT EYE DAMAGE.

INSTRUCTIONS: SEE DETAILED INSTRUCTIONS ON THE REVERSE SIDE OF THIS PAGE.

PAGE A

SOLAR ECLIPSE VIEWING DEVICE

INSTRUCTIONS:
1. CUT OUT PAGES 133 AND 135 ALONG DOTTED LINES.
2. ON PAGE A, CUT OUT THE SQUARE ALONG THE DOTTED LINES.
3. TAPE A PIECE OF FOIL OVER THE SQUARE.
4. USING A NEEDLE, POKE A SMALL HOLE IN THE MIDDLE OF THE FOIL.
5. WITH THE ECLIPSE BEHIND YOU, HOLD PAGE A IN THE AIR OVER PAGE B
   SO THAT THE PINHOLE PROJECTS AN IMAGE. THE ECLIPSE WILL BE
   VISIBLE ON PAGE B.

USE THE DIAGRAM ON THE REVERSE SIDE OF THIS PAGE TO CONSTRUCT THE VIEWING DEVICE. PROJECT THE IMAGE ON THE WHITE SIDE.

PAGE Ⓑ

SOLAR ECLIPSE VIEWING DEVICE

PROJECT THE IMAGE ON THE REVERSE SIDE OF THIS PAGE.

USE THESE DICE TO PREDICT YOUR FUTURE.

INSTRUCTIONS: CUT OUT ALONG THE DOTTED LINES. FOLD AS INDI-
CATED AND GLUE OR TAPE EDGES TOGETHER SO THAT YOU HAVE TWO
EIGHT-SIDED DICE. ROLL THE DICE AND SEE WHAT THEY TELL YOU.

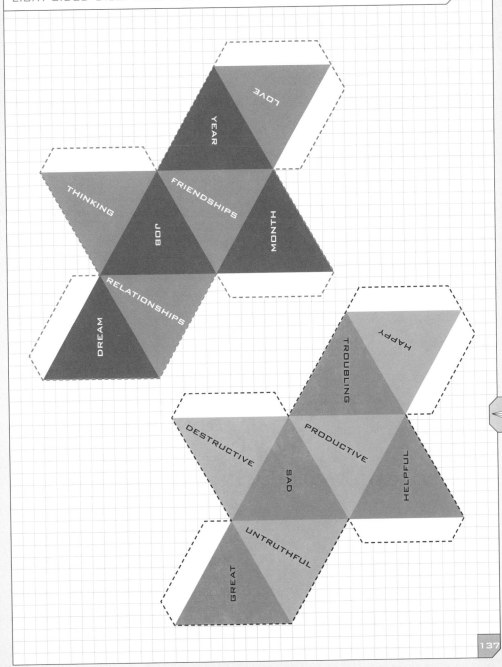

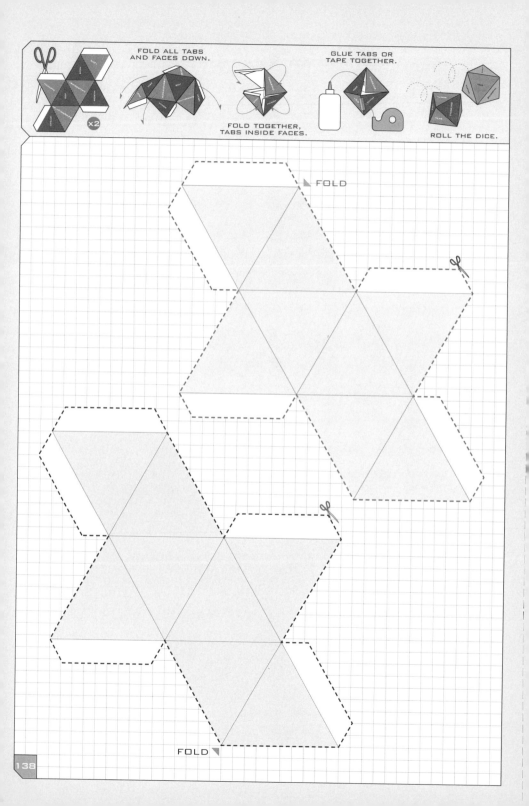

FOLD ALL TABS
AND FACES DOWN.

GLUE TABS OR
TAPE TOGETHER.

x2

FOLD TOGETHER,
TABS INSIDE FACES.

ROLL THE DICE.

FOLD

FOLD

FOLD

138

USE THIS DEVICE WHEN YOU NEED QUICK ANSWERS TO YOUR QUESTIONS.

INSTRUCTIONS: DETACH THE PAGE AND LAY IT ON A FLAT SURFACE. ASK YOUR QUESTION, AND THEN SPIN A COIN (NOT INCLUDED) ONTO THE PAGE. WHEREVER IT LANDS IS YOUR ANSWER.

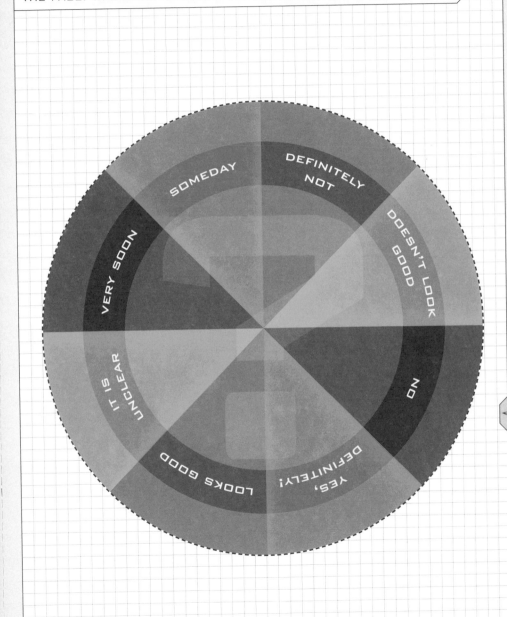

USE THIS DEVICE TO DETERMINE THE STATUS OF A RELATIONSHIP.

INSTRUCTIONS: SPIN A COIN ONTO THE PAGE. WHEREVER IT STOPS IS YOUR ANSWER. IF THE COIN LANDS OFF THE CHART, USE THE CLOSEST RESPONSE.

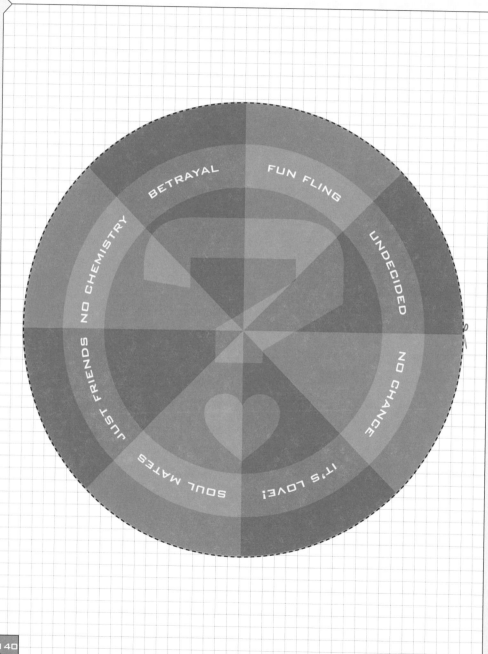

USE THIS DEVICE TO ENTERTAIN YOUR FRIENDS.

INSTRUCTIONS: CUT OUT SQUARE ALONG DOTTED LINES. SEE CONSTRUCTION INSTRUCTIONS ON THE REVERSE SIDE OF THIS PAGE.

HOW TO PLAY: HAVE A PLAYER CHOOSE A SHAPE. OPEN AND CLOSE THE COOTIE CATCHER ONE TIME FOR EVERY LETTER OF THAT SHAPE'S NAME. THEN HAVE THE PLAYER CHOOSE A NUMBER; OPEN AND CLOSE THE CATCHER THAT NUMBER OF TIMES. THE PLAYER THEN SELECTS ONE OF THE FOUR VISIBLE FLAPS. OPEN THE FLAP AND READ HIS OR HER FORTUNE.

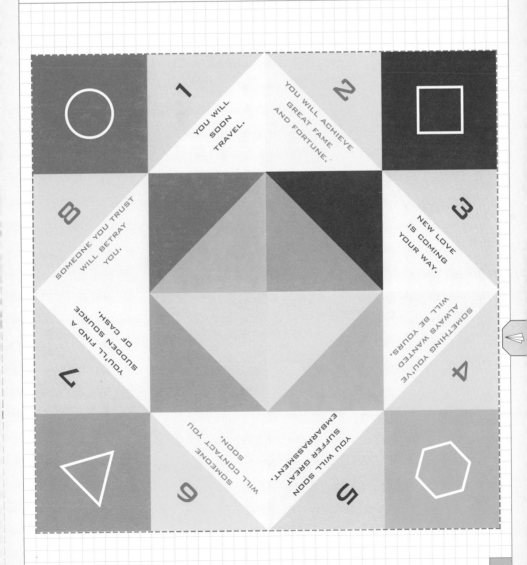

1

2

YOU WILL SOON TRAVEL.

YOU WILL ACHIEVE GREAT FAME AND FORTUNE.

8

3

SOMEONE YOU TRUST WILL BETRAY YOU.

NEW LOVE IS COMING YOUR WAY.

YOU'LL FIND A SUDDEN SOURCE OF CASH.

SOMETHING YOU'VE ALWAYS WANTED WILL BE YOURS.

7

4

6

5

YOU WILL SOON SUFFER GREAT EMBARRASSMENT.

SOMEONE WILL CONTACT YOU SOON.

141

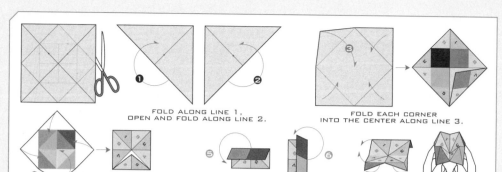

FOLD ALONG LINE 1,
OPEN AND FOLD ALONG LINE 2.

FOLD EACH CORNER
INTO THE CENTER ALONG LINE 3.

FLIP OVER
AND FOLD EACH CORNER
INTO THE CENTER ALONG LINE 4.

FOLD IN HALF HORIZONTALLY;
OPEN AND FOLD VERTICALLY.

WITH NUMBER SIDE UP,
INSERT THUMBS AND FINGERS.

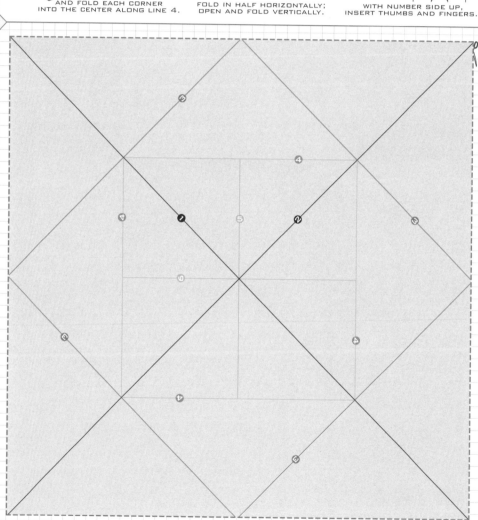

USE THIS CHART WHEN YOU WANT TO DETERMINE YOUR OR ANOTHER PERSON'S FUTURE.

INSTRUCTIONS: CUT OUT CHART ALONG DOTTED LINES. LOOK AT THE LEFT PALM. INTERPRET THE LINES: SHORT, LESS-DEFINED LINES INDICATE WEAKNESSES (FOR INSTANCE, A SHORT LIFE LINE COULD WARN OF A SHORT LIFE), A LONG AND WELL DEFINED LINE IS A POSITIVE SIGN.

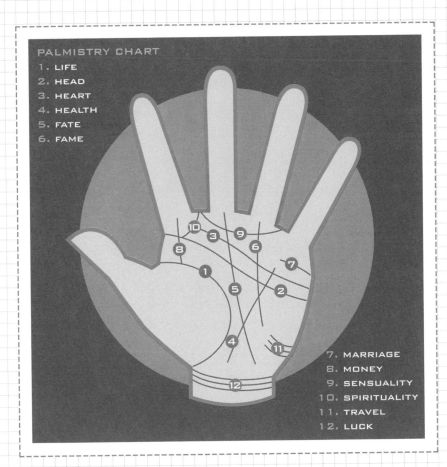

PALMISTRY CHART
1. LIFE
2. HEAD
3. HEART
4. HEALTH
5. FATE
6. FAME

7. MARRIAGE
8. MONEY
9. SENSUALITY
10. SPIRITUALITY
11. TRAVEL
12. LUCK

PALM READING ISN'T THE ONLY WAY TO FORETELL THE FUTURE. FOR ANOTHER FORTUNE-TELLING DEVICE, TURN TO PAGE 137.

USE THESE CARDS TO DETERMINE YOUR PSYCHIC ABILITIES.

INSTRUCTIONS: CUT OUT CARDS ALONG THE DOTTED LINES. THIS TEST REQUIRES TWO PEOPLE; ONE PERSON IS THE TESTER, THE OTHER THE TEST SUBJECT. THE TESTER SHOULD HOLD UP ONE CARD AT A TIME SO THAT THE PATTERN ON THE CARD IS NOT VISIBLE TO THE TEST SUBJECT. THE TEST SUBJECT GUESSES WHAT PATTERN IS ON THE CARD. THE TESTER SHOULD WRITE DOWN EACH CORRECT GUESS.

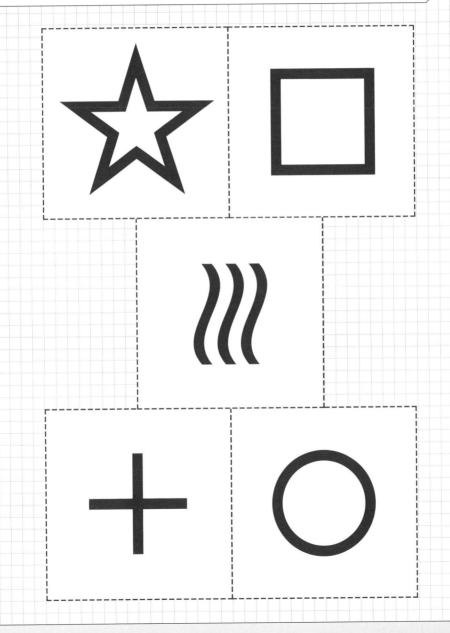

FIVE CORRECT OUT OF 25 IS CONSIDERED NORMAL CHANCE. ANYTHING OVER 9 SIGNIFIES PSYCHIC ABILITIES.

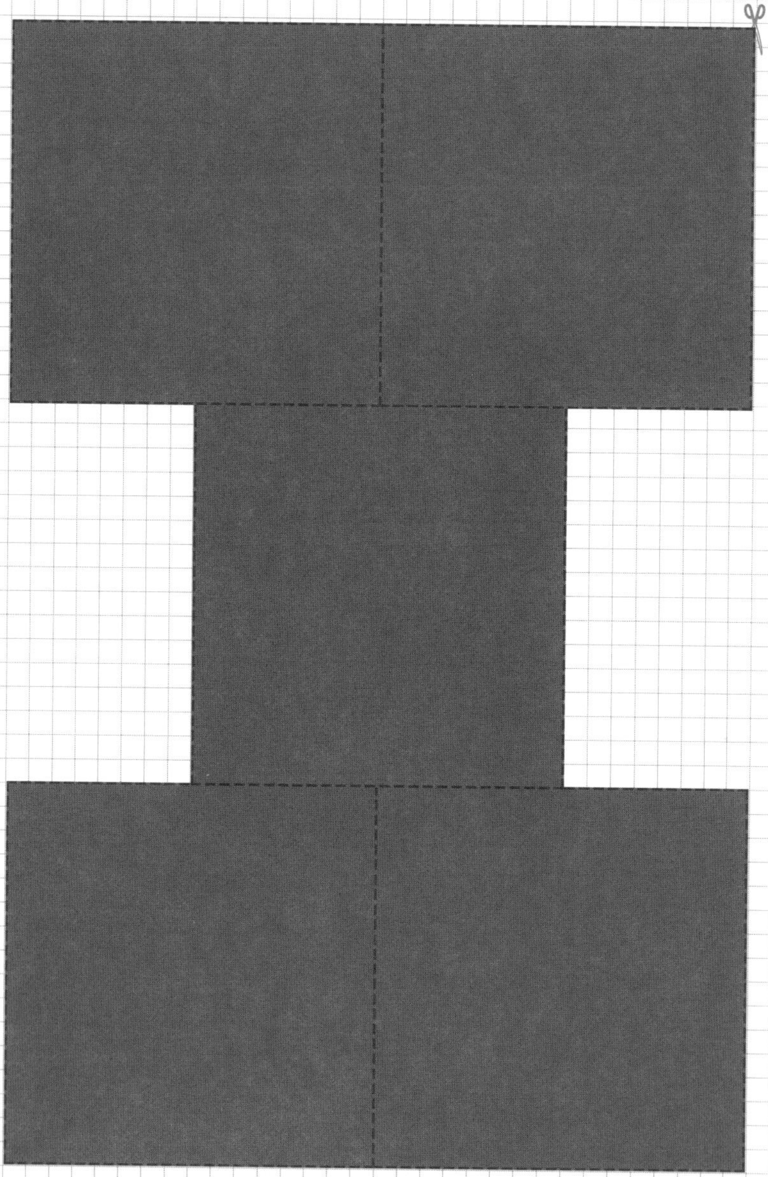

USE THIS LIST WHEN YOU'RE STUMPED IN A GAME OF SCRABBLE.

Z

INSTRUCTIONS: CUT ALONG DOTTED LINES AND KEEP WITH YOU DURING SCRABBLE GAMES.

TWO-LETTER WORDS ARE MOST USEFUL AT THE END OF THE GAME, WHEN YOU DON'T HAVE MANY OTHER OPTIONS.

APPROVED TWO-LETTER WORDS FOR SCRABBLE

AA	BI	HA	MI	OS	UP
AB	BO	HE	MM	OW	US
AD	BY	HI	MO	OX	UT
AE	DE	HM	MU	OY	WE
AG	DO	HO	MY	PA	WO
AH	ED	ID	NA	PE	XI
AL	EF	IF	NE	PI	XU
AM	EH	IN	NO	RE	YA
AN	EL	IS	NU	SH	YE
AR	EM	IT	OD	SI	YO
AS	EN	JO	OE	SO	
AT	ER	KA	OF	TA	
AW	ES	LA	OH	TI	
AX	ET	LI	OM	TO	
AY	EX	LO	ON	UH	
BA	FA	MA	OP	UM	
BE	GO	ME	OR	UN	

USE THESE WORDS WHEN YOU WANT TO SCORE HIGH POINTS IN SCRABBLE WITH "J," "Q," "X," AND "Z" WORDS.

"J" TWO- AND THREE-LETTER WORDS

JO	JAM	JET	JOB	JUG
HAJ	JAR	JEW	JOE	JUS
JAB	JAW	JIB	JOG	JUT
JAG	JAY	JIG	JOT	RAJ
JAK	JEE	JIN	JOY	TAJ

"J" FOUR-LETTER WORDS

DOJO	JARS	JEST	JINN	JOWL	JUNK
FUJI	JAVA	JETE	JINX	JOYS	JUPE
JABS	JAWS	JETS	JOBS	JUBA	JURY
JADE	JAYS	JEWS	JOCK	JUBE	JUST
JAGG	JAZZ	JIBB	JOGS	JUDO	JUTS
JAGS	JEER	JIBE	JOIN	JUGA	MOJO
JAIL	JEEZ	JIBS	JOKE	JUGS	PUJA
JAMS	JELL	JIFF	JOLT	JUJU	RAJA
JARL	JERK	JIGS	JOTS	JUMP	

"Q" TWO- AND THREE-LETTER WORDS

QI	QAT	QUA	SUQ

"Q" FOUR-LETTER WORDS

AQUA	QOPH	QUAY	QUIN	QUIZ
QADI	QUAD	QUEY	QUIP	QUOD
QATS	QUAG	QUID	QUIT	SUQS

"X" TWO- AND THREE-LETTER WORDS

AX	DEX	LAX	NIX	PYX	TAX
OX	FAX	LEX	OXO	REX	TUX
XI	FIX	LOX	OXY	SAX	VEX
AXE	FOX	LUX	PAX	SEX	VOX
BOX	HEX	MAX	PIX	SIX	WAX
COX	KEX	MIX	POX	SOX	ZAX

"X" FOUR-LETTER WORDS

APEX	CRUX	FAUX	JINX	ONYX	TEXT
AXED	DOXY	FLAX	LUXE	ORYX	WAXY
AXES	EXAM	FLEX	LYNX	OXEN	XYST
AXIS	EXEC	FLUX	MAXI	PIXY	
AXLE	EXES	FOXY	MINX	ROUX	
BOXY	EXIT	HOAX	NEXT	SEXY	
COAX	EXPO	ILEX	NIXY	TAXI	

"Z" TWO- AND THREE-LETTER WORDS

EZ	COZ	ZAP	ZEK	ZIT
ADZ	FEZ	ZAX	ZIG	ZOA
AZO	WIZ	ZED	ZIN	ZOO
BIZ	ZAG	ZEE	ZIP	

"Z" FOUR-LETTER WORDS

AZAN	DOZE	JAZZ	QUIZ	ZAPS	ZING
BIZE	FAZE	JEEZ	RAZZ	ZEALZ	ZIPS
BOZO	FIZZ	LAZE	RITZ	EIN	ZITI
BUZZ	FUTZ	LAZY	SIZE	ZEKS	ZOIC
CHEZ	FUZZ	LUTZ	SPAZ	ZERO	ZONE
COZY	GAZE	MAZE	TZAR	ZEST	ZONK
CZAR	GEEZ	NAZI	WHIZ	ZETA	ZOOM
DAZE	HAZE	OOZE	ZAGS	ZIGS	ZOOS
DITZ	HAZY	PUTZ	ZANY	ZINC	ZYME

USE THIS GAME WHEN YOU WANT TO PLAY A FAST AND EASY GAME ON THE GO.

INSTRUCTIONS: CAREFULLY CUT OUT X'S AND O'S AND PLAY ON THE BOARD (YOU CAN DETACH BOARD OR LEAVE IN BOOK).

USE THIS AIRPLANE WHEN SENDING NOTES OR WHEN THE OCCASION CALLS FOR FLYING PAPER (SPORTING EVENTS, WORK BREAKS, ETC.).

INSTRUCTIONS: CUT OUT ALONG DOTTED LINES. FOLD ALONG SOLID LINES IN CHRONOLOGICAL ORDER. DECORATE AS DESIRED.

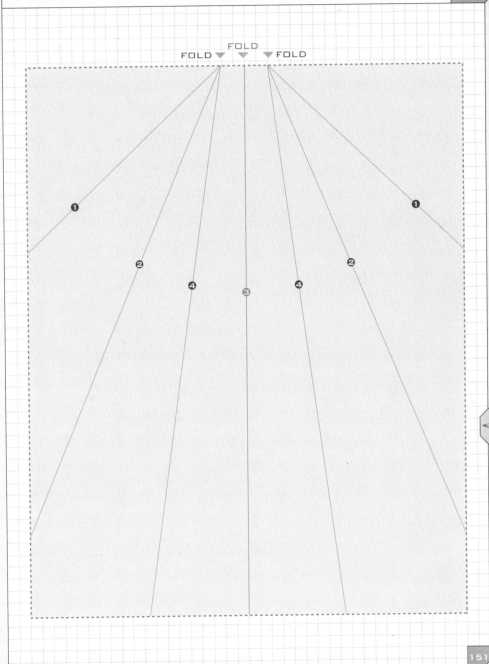

TO:

USE THIS SET TO PLAY CHESS WHEREVER YOU ARE.

INSTRUCTIONS: CUT OUT BOARD AND GAMEPIECES ALONG DOTTED RED LINES. FOLD GAMEPIECES ON SOLID BLUE LINE SO THEY STAND UPRIGHT. (ADDITIONAL CHESS PIECES ARE ON THE REVERSE SIDE OF THIS PAGE.)

TO USE AS A CHECKERBOARD: USE TWO DIFFERENT COINS AS GAMEPIECES.

FOLD ▶

FOLD ▶

USE THIS MAP WHEN YOU WANT TO LOCATE A COUNTRY AND DETERMINE ITS TIME.

INSTRUCTIONS: CUT OUT MAP ALONG DOTTED LINE.

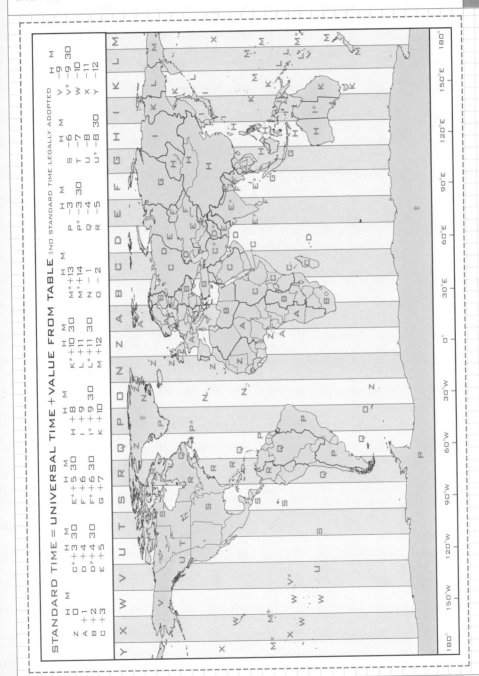

STANDARD TIME = UNIVERSAL TIME + VALUE FROM TABLE †NO STANDARD TIME LEGALLY ADOPTED

	H M		H M		H M		H M		H M		H M
Z	0	C*	+3 30	H	+8	M*+	+13	P	−3	V	−9
A	+1	D	+4	I	+9	M*+	+14	P*	−3 30	V*	−9 30
B	+2	D*	+4 30	I*	+9 30	N	−1	Q	−4	W	−10
C	+3	E	+5	K	+10	O	−2	R	−5	X	−11
		E*	+5 30	K*+	+10 30			S	−6	Y	−12
		F	+6	L	+11			T	−7		
		F*	+6 30	L*+	+11 30			U	−8		
		G	+7	M	+12			U*	−8 30		

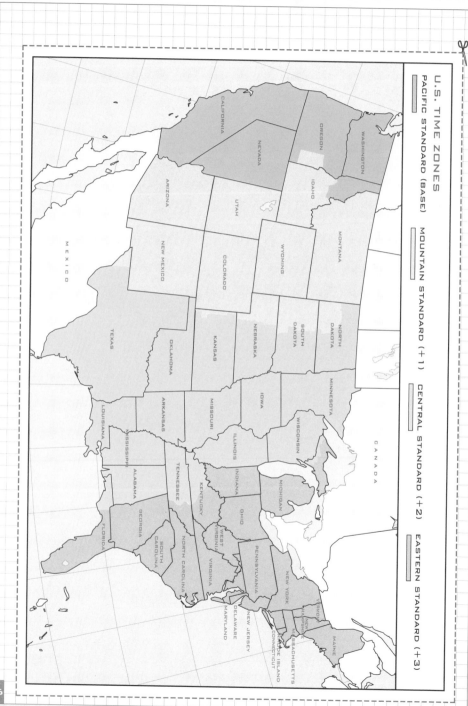

U.S. TIME ZONES

PACIFIC STANDARD (BASE)

MOUNTAIN STANDARD (+1)

CENTRAL STANDARD (+2)

EASTERN STANDARD (+3)

USE THIS SUN DIAL TO TELL THE TIME USING THE SHADOWS CREATED BY THE SUN.

INSTRUCTIONS: SEE DETAILED INSTRUCTIONS ON THE REVERSE SIDE OF THIS PAGE.

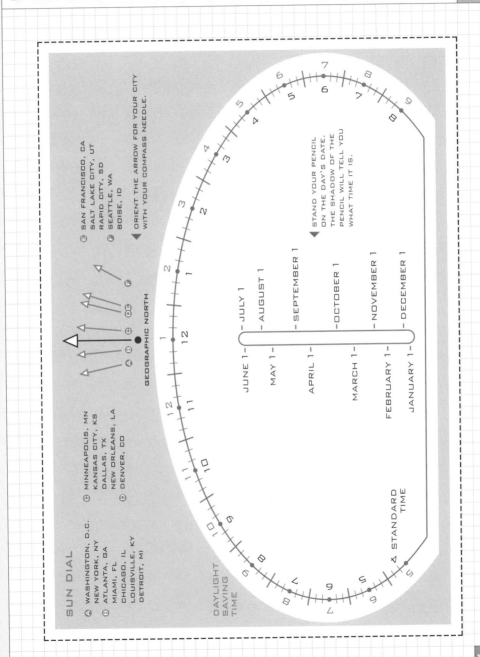

SUN DIAL

Ⓐ WASHINGTON, D.C.
NEW YORK, NY
ATLANTA, GA
MIAMI, FL
Ⓑ CHICAGO, IL
LOUISVILLE, KY
DETROIT, MI

Ⓒ MINNEAPOLIS, MN
KANSAS CITY, KS
DALLAS, TX
NEW ORLEANS, LA
Ⓓ DENVER, CO

Ⓔ SAN FRANCISCO, CA
SALT LAKE CITY, UT
RAPID CITY, SD
Ⓕ SEATTLE, WA
BOISE, ID

▼ ORIENT THE ARROW FOR YOUR CITY WITH YOUR COMPASS NEEDLE.

GEOGRAPHIC NORTH

▼ STAND YOUR PENCIL ON THE DAY'S DATE. THE SHADOW OF THE PENCIL WILL TELL YOU WHAT TIME IT IS.

JUNE 1 —
— JULY 1
MAY 1 —
— AUGUST 1
APRIL 1 —
— SEPTEMBER 1
— OCTOBER 1
MARCH 1 —
— NOVEMBER 1
FEBRUARY 1 —
— DECEMBER 1
JANUARY 1 —

DAYLIGHT SAVING TIME

⚹ STANDARD TIME

INSTRUCTIONS: CUT OUT ALONG DOTTED LINES.

1. USE A COMPASS (NOT INCLUDED) TO DETERMINE GEOGRAPHIC NORTH.

2. LAY THE SUN DIAL ON THE GROUND AND LINE UP THE ARROW FOR YOUR CITY WITH THE ARROW ON YOUR COMPASS.

3. STAND A PENCIL ON THE DAY'S DATE. THE SHADOW OF THE PENCIL WILL TELL YOU WHAT TIME IT IS!

IF YOU OUTSIDE OF THE U.S. OR ARE IN A CITY NOT LISTED BELOW, YOU CAN STILL USE THE SUN CLOCK. AT NIGHT, DETERMINE GEOGRAPHIC NORTH BY FINDING THE NORTH STAR. DRAW AN ARROW ON THE GROUND POINTING TOWARD THIS STAR. IN DAYLIGHT, LINE UP THE GEOGRAPHIC NORTH ARROW ON THE DIAL WITH THE ARROW YOU'VE DRAWN ON THE GROUND. CONTINUE WITH STEP 3.

USE THIS GUIDE WHEN YOU NEED TO IDENTIFY AN INCOMING CALL OR WHEN YOU NEED TO CALL INFORMATION (AREA CODE + 555-) FOR A PARTICULAR CITY IN THE U.S., CARIBBEAN, OR CANADA.

INSTRUCTIONS: DETACH AND PLACE NEAR TELEPHONE.

AREA CODES (U.S., CARIBBEAN, AND CANADA)

1 OF 4

011 INTERNATIONAL ACCESS
200 SERVICE ACCESS CODE
201 NEW JERSEY (NORTHEAST)
202 DISTRICT OF COLUMBIA
203 CONNECTICUT (SOUTHWEST)
204 MANITOBA
205 ALABAMA (BIRMINGHAM/ CENTRAL ALABAMA)
206 WASHINGTON (SEATTLE)
207 MAINE
208 IDAHO
209 CALIFORNIA (CENTRAL)
210 TEXAS (SAN ANTONIO)
211 COIN PHONE REFUNDS
212 NEW YORK (MANHATTAN)
213 CALIFORNIA (LOS ANGELES)
214 TEXAS (DALLAS)
215 PENNSYLVANIA (SOUTHEAST)
216 OHIO (CLEVELAND)
217 ILLINOIS (SOUTH CENTRAL)
218 MINNESOTA
219 INDIANA (NORTH)
224 ILLINOIS (NORTHEAST)
225 LOUISIANA (CENTRAL)
227 MARYLAND (SOUTH CENTRAL)
228 MISSISSIPPI (SOUTH)
229 GEORGIA (SOUTHWEST)
231 MICHIGAN (WEST)
234 OHIO (NORTHEAST)
239 FLORIDA (SOUTHWEST)
240 MARYLAND
242 BAHAMAS (CARIBBEAN)
246 BARBADOS (CARIBBEAN)
248 MICHIGAN (OAKLAND COUNTY)
250 BRITISH COLUMBIA
251 ALABAMA (SOUTHWEST CORNER)
252 NORTH CAROLINA (EAST)
253 WASHINGTON (TACOMA)
254 TEXAS (FT. WORTH)
256 ALABAMA (HUNTSVILLE/NORTH ALABAMA)
260 INDIANA (NORTH CENTRAL)
262 WISCONSIN (SOUTHEAST)
264 ANGUILLA
267 PENNSYLVANIA (PHILADELPHIA)
268 ANTIGUA/BARBUDA (CARIBBEAN)
269 MICHIGAN (SOUTHWEST)
270 KENTUCKY (WEST)

276 VIRGINIA (WEST)
278 MICHIGAN
281 TEXAS (HOUSTON)
283 OHIO (SOUTHEAST)
284 BRITISH VIRGIN ISLANDS
289 ONTARIO
300 SERVICE ACCESS CODE
301 MARYLAND (SOUTH AND WEST)
302 DELAWARE
303 COLORADO (DENVER & SUBURBS)
304 WEST VIRGINIA
305 FLORIDA (SOUTHEAST)
306 SASKATCHEWAN
307 WYOMING
308 NEBRASKA (WEST)
309 ILLINOIS (WEST CENTRAL)
310 CALIFORNIA (LOS ANGELES)
311 RESERVED SPECIAL FUNCTION
312 ILLINOIS (CHICAGO)
313 MICHIGAN (EAST)
314 MISSOURI (EAST)
315 NEW YORK (NORTH CENTRAL)
316 KANSAS (WICHITA AREA)
317 INDIANA (CENTRAL)
318 LOUISIANA (WEST)
319 IOWA (EAST)
320 MINNESOTA
321 FLORIDA SPACE COAST (MELBOURNE)
323 CALIFORNIA (LOS ANGELES)
325 TEXAS (CENTRAL)
330 OHIO (NORTHEAST)
331 ILLINOIS (NORTHEAST)
334 ALABAMA (MONTGOMERY/MOBILE/ LOWER ALABAMA)
336 NORTH CAROLINA (NORTH CENTRAL)
337 LOUISIANA (WEST)
339 MASSACHUSETTS (EAST)
340 US VIRGIN ISLANDS
341 CALIFORNIA (NORTH)
345 CAYMAN ISLANDS
347 NEW YORK (BROOKLYN/BRONX/ QUEENS/STATEN ISLAND)
351 MASSACHUSETTS (NORTHEAST)
352 FLORIDA (NORTH CENTRAL)
360 WASHINGTON (WEST)
361 TEXAS (SOUTHEAST)

CONTINUED FROM PAGE 159

369 CALIFORNIA (NORTHWEST)
386 FLORIDA (NORTH)
400 SERVICE ACCESS CODE
401 RHODE ISLAND
402 NEBRASKA (EAST)
403 ALBERTA (SOUTH)
404 GEORGIA (ATLANTA AREA)
405 OKLAHOMA (CENTRAL)
406 MONTANA
407 FLORIDA (ORLANDO AREA)
408 CALIFORNIA (CENTRAL COAST)
409 TEXAS (SOUTHEAST)
410 MARYLAND (EAST)
411 DIRECTORY SERVICES
412 PENNSYLVANIA (PITTSBURGH)
413 MASSACHUSETTS (WEST)
414 WISCONSIN (EAST)
415 CALIFORNIA (SAN FRANCISCO)
416 ONTARIO (TORONTO)
417 MISSOURI (SOUTHWEST)
418 QUEBEC (NORTHEAST)
419 OHIO (NORTHWEST)
423 TENNESSEE (EAST)
425 WASHINGTON (SEATTLE)
430 TEXAS (NORTHEAST)
432 TEXAS (WEST)
434 VIRGINIA (CENTRAL)
435 UTAH (ENTIRE STATE EXCEPT SALT
        LAKE CITY/PROVO REGION)
438 QUEBEC
440 OHIO (NORTHEAST)
441 BERMUDA (CARIBBEAN)
443 MARYLAND (EAST)
445 PENNSYLVANIA
450 QUEBEC (MONTREAL NORTH)
464 ILLINOIS
469 TEXAS (DALLAS)
470 GEORGIA (ATLANTA AREA)
473 GRENADA (CARIBBEAN)
475 CONNECTICUT
478 GEORGIA (CENTRAL)
479 ARKANSAS (WEST)
480 ARIZONA (CENTRAL)
484 PENNSYLVANIA (SOUTHEAST)
500 PERSONAL COMMUNICATION
        SERVICES
501 ARKANSAS (CENTRAL)
502 KENTUCKY (WEST)
503 OREGON (NORTHWEST)

504 LOUISIANA (EAST)
505 NEW MEXICO
506 NEW BRUNSWICK
507 MINNESOTA (SOUTH)
508 MASSACHUSETTS (EAST)
509 WASHINGTON (EAST)
510 CALIFORNIA (EAST BAY AREA)
512 TEXAS (SOUTH)
513 OHIO (SOUTHWEST)
514 QUEBEC (MONTREAL)
515 IOWA (CENTRAL)
516 NEW YORK (NASSAU COUNTY,
        LONG ISLAND)
517 MICHIGAN (SOUTH)
518 NEW YORK (NORTHEAST)
519 ONTARIO (SOUTHWEST)
520 ARIZONA (SOUTH)
530 CALIFORNIA (NORTH)
540 VIRGINIA (NORTHWEST)
541 OREGON (CENTRAL AND SOUTH)
551 NEW JERSEY (NORTHEAST)
557 MISSOURI (ST. LOUIS)
559 CALIFORNIA (CENTRAL)
561 FLORIDA (GREATER PALM BEACH)
562 CALIFORNIA (LOS ANGELES)
563 IOWA (NORTHEAST)
564 WASHINGTON
567 OHIO (NORTHWEST)
570 PENNSYLVANIA (NORTHEAST)
571 VIRGINIA (NORTH)
573 MISSOURI (SOUTHEAST)
574 INDIANA (SORTHEAST)
580 OKLAHOMA (WEST)
585 NEW YORK (WEST)
586 MICHIGAN (EAST)
600 CANADA GOVERNMENT
        SERVICES
601 MISSISSIPPI (CENTRAL)
602 ARIZONA (CENTRAL)
603 NEW HAMPSHIRE
604 BRITISH COLUMBIA
605 SOUTH DAKOTA
606 KENTUCKY (EAST)
607 NEW YORK (SOUTH CENTRAL)
608 WISCONSIN (SOUTHWEST)
609 NEW JERSEY (SOUTH)
610 PENNSYLVANIA (PHILADELPHIA
        SUBURBS/DELAWARE COUNTY)
611 REPAIR SERVICE

CONTINUED FROM PAGE 160

612 MINNESOTA (MINNEAPOLIS)
613 ONTARIO (SOUTHEAST)
614 OHIO (COLUMBUS AREA)
615 TENNESSEE (NASHVILLE)
616 MICHIGAN (WEST)
617 MASSACHUSETTS (BOSTON)
618 ILLINOIS (SOUTH)
619 CALIFORNIA (SAN DIEGO)
620 KANSAS (SOUTH)
623 ARIZONA (PHOENIX)
626 CALIFORNIA (PASADENA/
    SAN GABRIEL VALLEY)
627 CALIFORNIA (SANTA ROSA)
628 CALIFORNIA (SAN FRANCISCO)
630 ILLINOIS (CHICAGO SUBURBS)
631 NEW YORK (SUFFOLK COUNTY
    LONG ISLAND)
636 MISSOURI (EAST EXCLUDING
    ST. LOUIS)
641 IOWA (CENTRAL)
646 NEW YORK (MANHATTAN)
647 ONTARIO
649 TURKS AND CAICOS ISLANDS
650 CALIFORNIA (WEST BAY AREA)
651 MINNESOTA (ST. PAUL)
659 ALABAMA (BIRMINGHAM)
657 CALIFORNIA (ORANGE COUNTY/
    HUNTINGTON BEACH)
660 MISSOURI (CENTRAL)
661 CALIFORNIA (CENTRAL)
662 MISSISSIPPI (NORTH)
664 MONTSERRAT (CARIBBEAN)
667 MARYLAND (EAST)
669 CALIFORNIA (SAN JOSE)
670 CNMI (MARIANA ISLANDS)
671 GUAM
678 GEORGIA
679 MICHIGAN (DETROIT)
682 TEXAS (FT. WORTH)
689 FLORIDA (ORLANDO)
701 NORTH DAKOTA
702 NEVADA (SOUTH)
703 VIRGINIA (NORTH)
704 NORTH CAROLINA (WEST)
705 ONTARIO (NORTH)
706 GEORGIA (NORTH)
707 CALIFORNIA (NORTH COAST)
708 ILLINOIS (CHICAGO AREA)
709 NEWFOUNDLAND, LABRADOR

712 IOWA (WEST)
713 TEXAS (HOUSTON)
714 CALIFORNIA (ORANGE COUNTY)
715 WISCONSIN (NORTH)
716 NEW YORK (WEST)
717 PENNSYLVANIA (SOUTH CENTRAL)
718 NEW YORK (BROOKLYN/BRONX/
    QUEENS/STATEN ISLAND)
719 COLORADO (SOUTH AND EAST)
720 COLORADO (DENVER AND
    BOULDER AREAS)
724 PENNSYLVANIA (WEST)
727 FLORIDA (ST. PETERSBURG AND
    CLEARWATER)
731 TENNESSEE (WEST)
732 NEW JERSEY (EAST CENTRAL)
734 MICHIGAN (SOUTHEAST)
737 TEXAS (AUSTIN)
740 OHIO (SOUTHEAST)
747 CALIFORNIA (LOS ANGELES)
754 FLORIDA (BROWARD COUNTY)
757 VIRGINIA (EAST)
758 ST. LUCIA (CARIBBEAN)
760 CALIFORNIA (SAN DIEGO)
763 MINNESOTA (MINNEAPOLIS
    SUBURBS)
764 CALIFORNIA (SAN FRANCISCO)
765 INDIANA (CENTRAL)
767 DOMINICA
770 GEORGIA (ATLANTA AREA)
772 FLORIDA (EAST CENTRAL COAST)
773 ILLINOIS (CHICAGO)
774 MASSACHUSETTS (SOUTHEAST)
775 NEVADA (ENTIRE STATE EXCEPT
    LAS VEGAS AREA)
778 BRITISH COLUMBIA
780 ALBERTA, EDMONTON
781 MASSACHUSETTS (EAST)
784 ST. VINCENT/GRENADINES
785 KANSAS (NORTH)
786 FLORIDA (MIAMI)
787 PUERTO RICO (CARIBBEAN)
800 TOLL-FREE CALLING
801 UTAH (SALT LAKE CITY/PROVO)
802 VERMONT
803 SOUTH CAROLINA (CENTRAL)
804 VIRGINIA (SOUTHEAST)
805 CALIFORNIA (SOUTH CENTRAL)
806 TEXAS (NORTH PANHANDLE)

3 OF 4

807 ONTARIO (NORTHWEST)
808 HAWAII
809 CARIBBEAN ISLANDS
810 MICHIGAN (EAST)
812 INDIANA (SOUTH)
813 FLORIDA (TAMPA AREA)
814 PENNSYLVANIA (WEST/CENTRAL)
815 ILLINOIS (NORTH)
816 MISSOURI (NORTHWEST)
817 TEXAS (NORTH CENTRAL)
818 CALIFORNIA (LOS ANGELES AREA)
819 QUEBEC (EAST)
828 NORTH CAROLINA (WEST)
830 TEXAS (SOUTHWEST)
831 CALIFORNIA (CENTRAL COAST)
832 TEXAS (HOUSTON)
835 PENNSYLVANIA (DELAWARE/
        MONTGOMERY COUNTIES)
843 SOUTH CAROLINA (EAST)
845 NEW YORK (SOUTH)
847 ILLINOIS (CHICAGO SUBURBS)
848 NEW JERSEY (EAST)
850 FLORIDA (PANHANDLE)
856 NEW JERSEY (SOUTHWEST)
857 MASSACHUSETTS (BOSTON AREA)
858 CALIFORNIA (SAN DIEGO AREA)
859 KENTUCKY (CENTRAL)
860 CONNECTICUT (NORTH AND
        NORTHEAST)
862 NEW JERSEY (NORTH)
863 FLORIDA (SOUTH CENTRAL)
864 SOUTH CAROLINA (WEST)
865 TENNESSEE (EAST)
866 TOLL-FREE SERVICE
867 YUKON/NORTHWEST TERRITORY
868 TRINIDAD AND TOBAGO
        (CARIBBEAN)
869 ST. KITTS (CARIBBEAN)
870 ARKANSAS (EAST)
872 ILLINOIS (CHICAGO)
876 JAMAICA
877 TOLL-FREE CALLING
878 PENNSYLVANIA (WEST)
880 PAID 800 SERVICE
881 PAID 888 SERVICE
882 PAID 877 SERVICE
888 TOLL-FREE CALLING
900 VALUE ADDED INFO SVC CODE
901 TENNESSEE (WEST)

902 PRINCE EDWARD ISLAND,
        NOVA SCOTIA
903 TEXAS (NORTHEAST)
904 FLORIDA (NORTHEAST)
905 GREATER TORONTO AREA
        (EXCLUDING TORONTO)
906 MICHIGAN (NORTH)
907 ALASKA
908 NEW JERSEY (CENTRAL)
909 CALIFORNIA (RIVERSIDE AND SAN
        BERNADINO)
910 NORTH CAROLINA (SOUTH)
911 EMERGENCY SERVICES
912 GEORGIA (SOUTHEAST)
913 KANSAS (EAST)
914 NEW YORK (WESTCHESTER COUNTY)
915 TEXAS (WEST, BORDERING MEXICO)
916 CALIFORNIA (SACRAMENTO)
917 NEW YORK CITY
918 OKLAHOMA (NORTHEAST)
919 NORTH CAROLINA (EAST CENTRAL)
920 WISCONSIN (EAST)
925 CALIFORNIA (S. FRANCISCO BAY AREA)
928 ARIZONA (CENTRAL)
931 TENNESSEE (CENTRAL)
935 CALIFORNIA (SAN DIEGO)
936 TEXAS (EAST)
937 OHIO (WEST)
939 PUERTO RICO
940 TEXAS (FT. WORTH)
941 FLORIDA (CAPE CORAL AREA)
947 MICHIGAN (SOUTHEAST)
949 CALIFORNIA (ORANGE COUNTY)
951 CALIFORNIA (SOUTH)
952 MINNESOTA (MINNEAPOLIS SUBURBS)
954 FLORIDA (FT. LAUDERDALE AREA)
956 TEXAS (LAREDO/BROWNSVILLE)
959 CONNECTICUT (HARTFORD)
970 COLORADO (NORTH AND WEST)
971 OREGON (NORTHWEST)
972 TEXAS (DALLAS)
973 NEW JERSEY (NORTH)
975 MISSOURI (KANSAS CITY)
978 MASSACHUSETTS (NORTHEAST)
979 TEXAS (CENTRAL)
980 NORTH CAROLINA (WEST)
984 NORTH CAROLINA (RALEIGH)
985 LOUISIANA (SOUTHEAST)
989 MICHIGAN (NORTHEAST)

4 OF 4

USE THIS GUIDE WHEN YOU NEED TO IDENTIFY AN INCOMING CALL
OR WHEN YOU NEED TO CALL INFORMATION (AREA CODE + 555) FOR A
PARTICULAR CITY.

AREA CODES (U.S., CARIBBEAN, AND CANADA)

659	ALABAMA (BIRMINGHAM)		SAN GABRIEL VALLEY)
205	ALABAMA (BIRMINGHAM/ CENTRAL ALABAMA)	909	CALIFORNIA (RIVERSIDE AND SAN BERNADINO)
256	ALABAMA (HUNTSVILLE/ NORTH ALABAMA)	916	CALIFORNIA (SACRAMENTO)
		858	CALIFORNIA (SAN DIEGO AREA)
334	ALABAMA (MONTGOMERY/ MOBILE/LOWER ALABAMA)	619	CALIFORNIA (SAN DIEGO)
		760	CALIFORNIA (SAN DIEGO)
251	ALABAMA (SOUTHWEST CORNER)	935	CALIFORNIA (SAN DIEGO)
907	ALASKA	925	CALIFORNIA (SAN FRANCISCO BAY AREA)
403	ALBERTA (SOUTH)		
780	ALBERTA (EDMONTON)	415	CALIFORNIA (SAN FRANCISCO)
264	ANGUILLA	628	CALIFORNIA (SAN FRANCISCO)
268	ANTIGUA/BARBUDA (CARIBBEAN)	764	CALIFORNIA (SAN FRANCISCO)
480	ARIZONA (CENTRAL)	669	CALIFORNIA (SAN JOSE)
602	ARIZONA (CENTRAL)	627	CALIFORNIA (SANTA ROSA)
928	ARIZONA (CENTRAL)	805	CALIFORNIA (SOUTH CENTRAL)
623	ARIZONA (PHOENIX)	951	CALIFORNIA (SOUTH)
520	ARIZONA (SOUTH)	650	CALIFORNIA (WEST BAY AREA)
501	ARKANSAS (CENTRAL)	600	CANADA GOVERNMENT SERVICES
870	ARKANSAS (EAST)		
479	ARKANSAS (WEST)	809	CARIBBEAN ISLANDS
242	BAHAMAS (CARIBBEAN)	345	CAYMAN ISLANDS
246	BARBADOS (CARIBBEAN)	670	CNMI (MARIANA ISLANDS)
441	BERMUDA (CARIBBEAN)	211	COIN PHONE REFUNDS
250	BRITISH COLUMBIA	720	COLORADO (DENVER AND BOULDER AREAS)
604	BRITISH COLUMBIA		
778	BRITISH COLUMBIA	303	COLORADO (DENVER AND SUBURBS)
284	BRITISH VIRGIN ISLANDS	970	COLORADO (NORTH AND WEST)
408	CALIFORNIA (CENTRAL COAST)	719	COLORADO (SOUTH AND EAST)
831	CALIFORNIA (CENTRAL COAST)	475	CONNECTICUT
209	CALIFORNIA (CENTRAL)	959	CONNECTICUT (HARTFORD)
559	CALIFORNIA (CENTRAL)	860	CONNECTICUT (NORTH AND NORTHEAST)
661	CALIFORNIA (CENTRAL)		
510	CALIFORNIA (EAST BAY AREA)	203	CONNECTICUT (SOUTHWEST)
818	CALIFORNIA (LOS ANGELES AREA)	302	DELAWARE
213	CALIFORNIA (LOS ANGELES)	411	DIRECTORY SERVICES
310	CALIFORNIA (LOS ANGELES)	202	DISTRICT OF COLUMBIA
323	CALIFORNIA (LOS ANGELES)	767	DOMINICA
562	CALIFORNIA (LOS ANGELES)	911	EMERGENCY SERVICES
747	CALIFORNIA (LOS ANGELES)	754	FLORIDA (BROWARD COUNTY)
707	CALIFORNIA (NORTH COAST)	941	FLORIDA (CAPE CORAL AREA)
341	CALIFORNIA (NORTH)	772	FLORIDA (EAST CENTRAL COAST)
530	CALIFORNIA (NORTH)	954	FLORIDA (FT. LAUDERDALE AREA)
369	CALIFORNIA (NORTHWEST)	561	FLORIDA (GREATER PALM BEACH)
714	CALIFORNIA (ORANGE COUNTY)	786	FLORIDA (MIAMI)
949	CALIFORNIA (ORANGE COUNTY)	352	FLORIDA (NORTH CENTRAL)
657	CALIFORNIA (ORANGE COUNTY/ HUNTINGTON BEACH)	386	FLORIDA (NORTH)
		904	FLORIDA (NORTHEAST)
626	CALIFORNIA (PASADENA/	407	FLORIDA (ORLANDO AREA)

689	FLORIDA (ORLANDO)	913	KANSAS (EAST)
850	FLORIDA (PANHANDLE)	785	KANSAS (NORTH)
863	FLORIDA (SOUTH CENTRAL)	620	KANSAS (SOUTH)
305	FLORIDA (SOUTHEAST)	316	KANSAS (WICHITA AREA)
239	FLORIDA (SOUTHWEST)	859	KENTUCKY (CENTRAL)
727	FLORIDA (ST. PETERSBURG AND CLEARWATER)	606	KENTUCKY (EAST)
		502	KENTUCKY (WEST)
813	FLORIDA (TAMPA AREA)	270	KENTUCKY (WEST)
321	FLORIDA SPACE COAST (MELBOURNE)	225	LOUISIANA (CENTRAL)
		504	LOUISIANA (EAST)
678	GEORGIA	985	LOUISIANA (SOUTHEAST)
404	GEORGIA (ATLANTA AREA)	318	LOUISIANA (WEST)
470	GEORGIA (ATLANTA AREA)	337	LOUISIANA (WEST)
770	GEORGIA (ATLANTA AREA)	207	MAINE
478	GEORGIA (CENTRAL)	204	MANITOBA
706	GEORGIA (NORTH)	240	MARYLAND
912	GEORGIA (SOUTHEAST)	410	MARYLAND (EAST)
229	GEORGIA (SOUTHWEST)	443	MARYLAND (EAST)
905	GREATER TORONTO AREA (EXCLUDING TORONTO)	667	MARYLAND (EAST)
		301	MARYLAND (SOUTH AND WEST)
473	GRENADA (CARIBBEAN)	227	MARYLAND (SOUTH CENTRAL)
671	GUAM	857	MASSACHUSETTS (BOSTON AREA)
808	HAWAII	617	MASSACHUSETTS (BOSTON)
208	IDAHO	339	MASSACHUSETTS (EAST)
464	ILLINOIS	508	MASSACHUSETTS (EAST)
708	ILLINOIS (CHICAGO AREA)	781	MASSACHUSETTS (EAST)
630	ILLINOIS (CHICAGO SUBURBS)	351	MASSACHUSETTS (NORTHEAST)
847	ILLINOIS (CHICAGO SUBURBS)	978	MASSACHUSETTS (NORTHEAST)
312	ILLINOIS (CHICAGO)	774	MASSACHUSETTS (SOUTHEAST)
773	ILLINOIS (CHICAGO)	413	MASSACHUSETTS (WEST)
872	ILLINOIS (CHICAGO)	278	MICHIGAN
815	ILLINOIS (NORTH)	679	MICHIGAN (DETROIT)
224	ILLINOIS (NORTHEAST)	313	MICHIGAN (EAST)
331	ILLINOIS (NORTHEAST)	586	MICHIGAN (EAST)
217	ILLINOIS (SOUTH CENTRAL)	810	MICHIGAN (EAST)
618	ILLINOIS (SOUTH)	906	MICHIGAN (NORTH)
309	ILLINOIS (WEST CENTRAL)	989	MICHIGAN (NORTHEAST)
317	INDIANA (CENTRAL)	248	MICHIGAN (OAKLAND CITY)
765	INDIANA (CENTRAL)	517	MICHIGAN (SOUTH)
260	INDIANA (NORTH CENTRAL)	734	MICHIGAN (SOUTHEAST)
219	INDIANA (NORTH)	947	MICHIGAN (SOUTHEAST)
574	INDIANA (NORTHEAST)	269	MICHIGAN (SOUTHWEST)
812	INDIANA (SOUTH)	616	MICHIGAN (WEST)
011	INTERNATIONAL ACCESS	231	MICHIGAN (WEST)
515	IOWA (CENTRAL)	218	MINNESOTA
641	IOWA (CENTRAL)	320	MINNESOTA
319	IOWA (EAST)	763	MINNESOTA (MINNEAPOLIS SUBURBS)
563	IOWA (NORTHEAST)		
712	IOWA (WEST)	952	MINNESOTA (MINNEAPOLIS SUBURBS)
876	JAMAICA		

CONTINUED FROM PAGE 164

612 MINNESOTA (MINNEAPOLIS)	914 NEW YORK (WESTCHESTER COUNTY)
507 MINNESOTA (SOUTH)	917 NEW YORK CITY
651 MINNESOTA (ST. PAUL)	709 NEWFOUNDLAND, LABRADOR
601 MISSISSIPPI (CENTRAL)	919 NORTH CAROLINA (EAST CENTRAL)
662 MISSISSIPPI (NORTH)	252 NORTH CAROLINA (EAST)
228 MISSISSIPPI (SOUTH)	336 NORTH CAROLINA (NORTH CENTRAL)
660 MISSOURI (CENTRAL)	
636 MISSOURI (EAST EXCLUDING ST. LOUIS)	984 NORTH CAROLINA (RALEIGH)
314 MISSOURI (EAST)	910 NORTH CAROLINA (SOUTH)
975 MISSOURI (KANSAS CITY)	704 NORTH CAROLINA (WEST)
816 MISSOURI (NORTHWEST)	828 NORTH CAROLINA (WEST)
573 MISSOURI (SOUTHEAST)	980 NORTH CAROLINA (WEST)
417 MISSOURI (SOUTHWEST)	701 NORTH DAKOTA
557 MISSOURI (ST. LOUIS)	216 OHIO (CLEVELAND)
406 MONTANA	614 OHIO (COLUMBUS AREA)
664 MONTSERRAT (CARIBBEAN)	234 OHIO (NORTHEAST)
402 NEBRASKA (EAST)	330 OHIO (NORTHEAST)
308 NEBRASKA (WEST)	440 OHIO (NORTHEAST)
775 NEVADA (ENTIRE STATE EXCEPT LAS VEGAS AREA)	419 OHIO (NORTHWEST)
	567 OHIO (NORTHWEST)
702 NEVADA (SOUTH)	283 OHIO (SOUTHEAST)
506 NEW BRUNSWICK	740 OHIO (SOUTHEAST)
603 NEW HAMPSHIRE	513 OHIO (SOUTHWEST)
908 NEW JERSEY (CENTRAL)	937 OHIO (WEST)
732 NEW JERSEY (EAST CENTRAL)	405 OKLAHOMA (CENTRAL)
848 NEW JERSEY (EAST)	918 OKLAHOMA (NORTHEAST)
862 NEW JERSEY (NORTH)	580 OKLAHOMA (WEST)
973 NEW JERSEY (NORTH)	289 ONTARIO
201 NEW JERSEY (NORTHEAST)	647 ONTARIO
551 NEW JERSEY (NORTHEAST)	705 ONTARIO (NORTH)
609 NEW JERSEY (SOUTH)	807 ONTARIO (NORTHWEST)
856 NEW JERSEY (SOUTHWEST)	613 ONTARIO (SOUTHEAST)
505 NEW MEXICO	519 ONTARIO (SOUTHWEST)
347 NEW YORK (BROOKLYN/BRONX/ QUEENS/STATEN ISLAND)	416 ONTARIO (TORONTO)
	541 OREGON (CENTRAL AND SOUTH)
718 NEW YORK (BROOKLYN/BRONX/ QUEENS/STATEN ISLAND)	503 OREGON (NORTHWEST)
	971 OREGON (NORTHWEST)
212 NEW YORK (MANHATTAN)	880 PAID 800 SERVICE
646 NEW YORK (MANHATTAN)	882 PAID 877 SERVICE
516 NEW YORK (NASSAU COUNTY, LONG ISLAND)	881 PAID 888 SERVICE
	445 PENNSYLVANIA
315 NEW YORK (NORTH CENTRAL)	484 PENNSYLVANIA (SOUTHEAST)
518 NEW YORK (NORTHEAST)	835 PENNSYLVANIA (DELAWARE/ MONTGOMERY COUNTIES)
607 NEW YORK (SOUTH CENTRAL)	
845 NEW YORK (SOUTH)	570 PENNSYLVANIA (NORTHEAST)
631 NEW YORK (SUFFOLK COUNTY, LONG ISLAND)	610 PENNSYLVANIA (PHILADELPHIA SUBURBS/DELAWARE COUNTY)
585 NEW YORK (WEST)	267 PENNSYLVANIA (PHILADELPHIA)
716 NEW YORK (WEST)	

412	PENNSYLVANIA (PITTSBURGH)	956	TEXAS (LAREDO/BROWNSVILLE)
717	PENNSYLVANIA (SOUTH CENTRAL)	817	TEXAS (NORTH CENTRAL)
215	PENNSYLVANIA (SOUTHEAST)	806	TEXAS (NORTH PANHANDLE)
724	PENNSYLVANIA (WEST)	430	TEXAS (NORTHEAST)
878	PENNSYLVANIA (WEST)	903	TEXAS (NORTHEAST)
814	PENNSYLVANIA (WEST/CENTRAL)	210	TEXAS (SAN ANTONIO)
500	PERSONAL COMMUNICATION SERVICES	512	TEXAS (SOUTH)
		361	TEXAS (SOUTHEAST)
902	PRINCE EDWARD ISLAND, NOVA SCOTIA	409	TEXAS (SOUTHEAST)
		830	TEXAS (SOUTHWEST)
939	PUERTO RICO	432	TEXAS (WEST)
787	PUERTO RICO (CARIBBEAN)	915	TEXAS (WEST, BORDERING MEXICO)
438	QUEBEC		
819	QUEBEC (EAST)	800	TOLL-FREE CALLING
450	QUEBEC (MONTREAL NORTH)	877	TOLL-FREE CALLING
514	QUEBEC (MONTREAL)	888	TOLL-FREE CALLING
418	QUEBEC (NORTHEAST)	866	TOLL-FREE SERVICE
611	REPAIR SERVICE	868	TRINIDAD AND TOBAGO (CARIBBEAN)
311	RESERVED SPECIAL FUNCTION		
401	RHODE ISLAND	649	TURKS AND CAICOS ISLANDS
306	SASKATCHEWAN	340	US VIRGIN ISLANDS
200	SERVICE ACCESS CODE	435	UTAH (ENTIRE STATE EXCEPT SALT LAKE CITY/PROVO REGION)
300	SERVICE ACCESS CODE		
400	SERVICE ACCESS CODE	801	UTAH (SALT LAKE CITY/PROVO)
803	SOUTH CAROLINA (CENTRAL)	900	VALUE ADDED INFO SVC CODE
843	SOUTH CAROLINA (EAST)	802	VERMONT
864	SOUTH CAROLINA (WEST)	434	VIRGINIA (CENTRAL)
605	SOUTH DAKOTA	757	VIRGINIA (EAST)
869	ST. KITTS (CARIBBEAN)	571	VIRGINIA (NORTH)
758	ST. LUCIA (CARIBBEAN)	703	VIRGINIA (NORTH)
784	ST. VINCENT/GRENADINES	540	VIRGINIA (NORTHWEST)
931	TENNESSEE (CENTRAL)	804	VIRGINIA (SOUTHEAST)
423	TENNESSEE (EAST)	276	VIRGINIA (WEST)
865	TENNESSEE (EAST)	564	WASHINGTON
615	TENNESSEE (NASHVILLE)	509	WASHINGTON (EAST)
731	TENNESSEE (WEST)	206	WASHINGTON (SEATTLE)
901	TENNESSEE (WEST)	425	WASHINGTON (SEATTLE)
737	TEXAS (AUSTIN)	253	WASHINGTON (TACOMA)
325	TEXAS (CENTRAL)	360	WASHINGTON (WEST)
979	TEXAS (CENTRAL)	304	WEST VIRGINIA (ENTIRE STATE)
214	TEXAS (DALLAS)	414	WISCONSIN (EAST)
469	TEXAS (DALLAS)	920	WISCONSIN (EAST)
972	TEXAS (DALLAS)	715	WISCONSIN (NORTH)
936	TEXAS (EAST)	262	WISCONSIN (SOUTHEAST)
682	TEXAS (FT. WORTH)	608	WISCONSIN (SOUTHWEST)
254	TEXAS (FT. WORTH)	307	WYOMING
940	TEXAS (FT. WORTH)	867	YUKON/NORTHWEST TERRITORY
281	TEXAS (HOUSTON)		
713	TEXAS (HOUSTON)		
832	TEXAS (HOUSTON)		

USE THESE CODES WHEN CALLING OUT OF THE COUNTRY.

INSTRUCTIONS: DETACH PAGE AND KEEP NEAR THE TELEPHONE. NOTE THAT DIALING INSTRUCTIONS VARY FROM COUNTRY TO COUNTRY. OFTEN, YOU MUST DIAL THE INTERNATIONAL ACCESS CODE (WHICH VARIES) + COUNTRY CODE + CITY CODE + LOCAL NUMBER.

INTERNATIONAL DIALING CODES

1 OF 4

	COUNTRY CODE	CITY CODES (IF BLANK, NOT REQUIRED)
AFGHANISTAN	930	
ALBANIA	255	ELBASSAN 545, TIRANA 42, DURRES 52
ANTIGUA	268*	
ARGENTINA	54	BUENOS AIRES 11, CORDOBA 351, SANTA FE 342
AUSTRALIA	61	CANBERRA 2, SYDNEY 2, MELBOURNE 3, ADELAIDE 8
AUSTRIA	43	SALZBURG 662, VIENNA 1, LINZ DONAU 70 OR 732
BAHAMAS	242*	
BARBADOS	246*	
BELGIUM	32	BRUSSELS 2, ANTWERP 3, GHENT 9
BELIZE	501	BELMOPAN 822, ORANGE WALK 322, BELIZE CITY 222
BERMUDA	441*	
BOSNIA	387	MOSTAR 36, SARAJEVO 33, ZENICA 32
BRAZIL	55	SALVADOR 71, BRASILIA 61, RIO DE JANEIRO 21, SAO PAULO 11
BRITISH VIRGIN IS.	284*	
CAYMAN IS.	345*	
CHILE	56	SANTIAGO 2, CONCEPCION 41, VALPARAISO 32
CHINA (NORTH)	86	HARBIN 451, SHENYANG 24, TAIYUAN 351, QINGDAO 532, BEIJING 10, JILIN 453, CHANGCHUN 431, JINAN 531, KAIFENG 378, HOHHOT 472, TIANJIN 22, DALIAN 411, ZHENGZHOU 371, SHIJIAZHUANG 311
CHINA (SOUTH)	86	GUILIN 773, XIAMEN 592, FUZHOU 591, CHENGDU 28, HANGZHOU 571, XIAN 29, SHENZHEN 755, ZHUHAI 756, GUANGZHOU 20, SUZHOU 557, NANJING 25, SHANGHAI 21
COLOMBIA	57	BOGOTA 1, MEDELLIN 4, CALI 2
COOK IS.	682	

	COUNTRY CODE	CITY CODES (IF BLANK, NOT REQUIRED)
COSTA RICA	506	
CUBA	53	ALL CITIES 99
CZECH REPUBLIC	420	PRAGUE 2, OSTRAVA 69, BRNO 5
DENMARK	45	
DOMINICA	767*	
DOMINICAN REP.	809*	
ECUADOR	593	GUAYAQUIL 4, QUITO 2, LOJA 7
EGYPT	20	ALEXANDRIA 3, CAIRO 2, ASYUT 88
EL SALVADOR	503	EL PARAISO 356, LA FONTERA (NOT REQUIRED), GUAZAPA 324, SAN MARTIN 25, OLOMEGA 121, APOPA 216, LOS LAGARTOS 121, SAN MIGUELITO 235
FIJI	679	
FINLAND	358	TURKU 2, VAASA 6, HELSINKI 9
FRANCE	33	
FRENCH POLYNESIA	689	
GERMANY	49	BERLIN 30, MUNICH 89, HAMBURG 40
GIBRALTAR	350	
GREECE	30	ATHENS 210, THESSALONIKI 2310, CRETE 2810
GREENLAND	299	
GRENADA	473*	
GUAM	671*	
GUATEMALA	502	
HAITI	509	
HONDURAS	504	
HONG KONG	852	
HUNGARY	36	SZOLNOK 56, BUDAPEST 1, VESZPREM 88
ICELAND	354	AKUREYRI 46, OTHER CITIES NOT REQUIRED
INDIA	91	BOMBAY 22, CALCUTTA 33, NEW DELHI 11
INDONESIA	62	JAKARTA 21, MEDAN 61, BANDUNG 22
IRAN	98	ESFAHAN 311, BAM 344, SHIRAZ 711, TEHRAN 212

2 OF 4

CONTINUED FROM PAGE 168

	COUNTRY CODE	CITY CODES (IF BLANK, NOT REQUIRED)
IRAQ	964	MOSUL 60, BAGHDAD 1, ARBIL 66, SULAIMANIYA 532
IRELAND	353	DUBLIN 1, CORK 21, DONEGAL 73
ISRAEL	972	NAZARETH 4, SAFED 4, JERUSALEM 2, EILAT 8, LOD 8, HAIFA 4, TEL AVIV 3
ITALY	39	NAPLES 081, FLORENCE 055, ROME 06
IVORY COAST	225	
JAMAICA	876*	
JAPAN	81	NAGOYA 52, OSAKA 6, TOKYO 3
KOREA	82	SEOUL 2, PUSAN 51, TAEGU 53
KUWAIT	965	
LITHUANIA	370	KLAIPEDA 46, VILNIUS 5, KAUNAS 37
MALAYSIA	60	JOHOR BAHRU 7, IPOH 5, KUALA LUMPUR 3
MEXICO	52	MONTERREY 81, MEXICO CITY 55, GUADALAJARA 33, ACAPULCO 744
MOROCCO	212	FES 55, RABAT 37, CASA BLANCA 22,
MARRAKECH	44	
MOZAMBIQUE	258	QUELIMANE 4, BEIRA 3, MATOLA 4, NAMPULA 6, MAPUTO 1
NAMIBIA	264	LUDERITZ 63, WINDHOEK 61, KEETMANSHOOP 63
NEPAL	977	POKHARA 61, KATHMANDU 1, PATAN 1, BHAKTAPUR 1
NETHERLANDS	31	AMSTERDAM 20, THE HAGUE 70, HAARLEM 23
NEW ZEALAND	64	AUCKLAND 9, WANGANUI 6, WELLINGTON 4
NICARAGUA	505	CHINANDEGA 341, LEON 311, MANAGUA 2
NORWAY	47	
PAKISTAN	92	LAHORE 42, KARACHI 21, ISLAMABAD 51
PANAMA	507	
PERU	51	LIMA 1, ARAQUIPA 54, PIURA 73
PHILIPPINES	63	CEBU CITY 32, DAVAO 82, MANILA 2
POLAND	48	GDANSK 58, KATOWICE 32, WARSAW 22
PORTUGAL	351	SETUBAL 265, LISBON 21, COIMBRA 239
PUERTO RICO	787* OR 939*	

3 OF 4

	COUNTRY CODE	CITY CODES (IF BLANK, NOT REQUIRED)
RUSSIA	7	ST. PETERSBURG 812, MOSCOW 095, MAGADAN 413
SAUDI ARABIA	966	RIYADH 1, MAKKAH (MECCA) 2, JEDDAH 2
SENEGAL	221	DAKAR 8, ALL OTHER 9
SINGAPORE	65	EAST 6, JURONG EAST 6, ORCHARD 6
SLOVENIA	386	KOBARID 5, LJUBLJANA DOBRUNJE 3, LJUTOMER 2, LJUBLJANA CRNUCE 1
SOUTH AFRICA	27	JOHANNESBURG 11, CAPE TOWN 21, PRETORIA 12, PIETERMARITZBURG 33
SPAIN	34	BARCELONA 93, MADRID 91, MALAGA 95
ST. KITTS	869*	
ST. LUCIA	758*	
SURINAME	597	
SWEDEN	46	GOTHENBURG 31, STOCKHOLM 8, MALMO 40
SWITZERLAND	41	ZURICH 1, LUCERNE 41, BERNE 31
TAIWAN	886	CHANGHUA 4, TAIPEI 2
TANZANIA	255	TANGA 27, ARUSHA 27, ZANZIBAR 24, DAR ES SALAAM 22
THAILAND	66	NAKHON SAWAN 56, BANGKOK 2, CHIANG MAI 53
TRINIDAD/ TOBAGO	868*	
TURKEY	90	ANKARA 312, IZMIR 232, ISTANBUL 212
TURKS AND CAICOS	649*	
UKRAINE	380	LVOV 32, KHARKIV 57, KIEV 44
UNITED KINGDOM	44	MANCHESTER 161, NOTTINGHAM 115, LONDON 20
UNITED STATES	1	SEE PAGE 159 FOR STATE AREA CODES
US VIRGIN ISLANDS	340*	
VENEZUELA	58	CARACAS 212, PUERTO CABELLO 242, CABIMAS 264
VIETNAM	84	HANOI 4, HO CHI MINH CITY 8
ZIMBABWE	263	BULAWAYO 9, HARARE 4, MUTARE 20

* THESE ARE AREA CODES UNDER THE NORTH AMERICAN NUMBERING PLAN AND CAN BE USED JUST LIKE U.S. AREA CODES.

USE THESE NUMBERS IN THE EVENT OF AN EMERGENCY WHILE ABROAD OR AT HOME.

INSTRUCTIONS: DETACH PAGE AND KEEP ON YOUR PERSON AT ALL TIMES IN CASE OF EMERGENCY. SEE PAGE 167 FOR RELEVANT COUNTRY AND AREA CODES.

IMPORTANT PHONE NUMBERS

ANGUILLA	911
ANTIGUA	999 OR 911
ARGENTINA	101
ARUBA	74-300 (AMBULANCE); 115 (FIRE); 11-000 (POLICE)
AUSTRALIA	000
AUSTRIA	144 (AMBULANCE); 122 (FIRE); 133 (POLICE)
BAHAMAS	911
BARBADOS	115 (AMBULANCE); 113 (FIRE); 112 (POLICE)
BELGIUM	100 (AMBULANCE OR FIRE); 101 (POLICE)
BELIZE	911
BERMUDA	911
BRAZIL	0
BRITISH VIRGIN ISLANDS	112 (AMBULANCE); 114 (POLICE)
CANADA	911
CAYMAN ISLANDS	555 (AMBULANCE); 911 (EMERGENCY & POLICE)
CHILE	132 (FIRE); 133 (POLICE)
CHINA	119 (FIRE); 110 (POLICE)
COOK ISLANDS	999 (POLICE); 998 (AMBULANCE)
COSTA RICA	225-1436 AND 228-2187 (AMBULANCE); 103 (FIRE); 104 (POLICE)
CYPRUS	199
CZECH REPUBLIC	155 (AMBULANCE); 150 (FIRE); 158 (POLICE)
DENMARK	112 (AMBULANCE AND POLICE IN COPENHAGEN)
DOMINICA	999
ECUADOR	131 (AMBULANCE); 101 (POLICE)
ENGLAND	999

FIJI	000
FINLAND	000 (AMBULANCE AND FIRE IN HELSINKI); 002 (POLICE IN HELSINKI)
FRANCE	15 (AMBULANCE); 18 (FIRE); 17 (POLICE)
GERMANY	112 (FIRE); 110 (POLICE)
GREECE	116 (AMBULANCE); 199 (FIRE); 100 (POLICE)
GUADELOUPE	18 (AMBULANCE AND FIRE); 17 (POLICE)
GUATEMALA	125 OR 128 (AMBULANCE); 122 OR 123 (FIRE); 120, 137 OR 138 (POLICE)
HONDURAS	37-8654 (AMBULANCE); 198 (FIRE); 119 (POLICE)
HONG KONG	999
HUNGARY	104 (AMBULANCE); 105 (FIRE); 107 (POLICE)
IRELAND	999
ISRAEL	101 (AMBULANCE); 100 (FIRE AND POLICE)
ITALY	113 (AMBULANCE); 115 (FIRE); 112 (POLICE)
JAMAICA	110 (AMBULANCE & FIRE); 119 (POLICE)
JAPAN	0120-461-997 (OPERATOR SERVICE)
JORDAN	193 (AMBULANCE & FIRE); 192 (POLICE)
KENYA	336886 OR 501280
LATVIA	03 (AMBULANCE); 01 (FIRE); 7219-310 (POLICE)
MACEDONIA	94 (AMBULANCE); 93 (FIRE); 92 (POLICE)
MALAYSIA	999
MALDIVES	102 (AMBULANCE); 118 (FIRE); 119 (POLICE)
MALTA	196 (AMBULANCE); 199 (FIRE); 191 (POLICE)
MEXICO	08
NAMIBIA	203-2276 (AMBULANCE); 203-2270 (FIRE); 1011 (POLICE)

FOLD ▼

FOLD ►

FOLD ►

NEW ZEALAND   111

NICARAGUA   265-1761 (AMBULANCE);
265-0162 (FIRE);
118 (POLICE)

NORTHERN IRELAND   999

NORWAY   003 (AMBULANCE);
002 (POLICE IN OSLO)

PANAMA   225-1436 OR
228-2187 (AMBULANCE);
103 (FIRE); 104 (POLICE)

PARAGUAY   00

PERU   011 OR 5114

POLAND   999 (AMBULANCE);
998 (FIRE); 997 (POLICE)

PORTUGAL   115

PUERTO RICO   911

ROMANIA   961 (AMBULANCE);
981 (FIRE); 955 (POLICE)

RUSSIA   03 (AMBULANCE);
01 (FIRE); 02 (POLICE)

SCOTLAND   999

SINGAPORE   999 (POLICE);
995 (AMBULANCE)

SOUTH AFRICA
10222 (AMBULANCE);
1022 (FIRE); 1011 (POLICE)

SPAIN   085 (AMBULANCE & FIRE);
091 (POLICE)

SRI LANKA   1-691095 OR
699935

ST. KITTS AND NEVIS
911

ST. LUCIA   999

ST. VINCENT AND GRENADINES
999

SWEDEN   90-000-112

SWITZERLAND
144 (AMBULANCE);
118 (FIRE); 117 (POLICE)

TAIWAN   110

THAILAND   191

THE NETHERLANDS
0611

TONGA ISLANDS   911

TRINIDAD AND TOBAGO
990 (AMBULANCE & FIRE);
9 (POLICE)

TURKS AND CAICOS ISLANDS
911

UNITED ARAB EMIRATES
344-663 (IN ABA DHABI)

UNITED STATES OF AMERICA
911

URUGUAY   999

VENEZUELA   02-545-4545 (AMBU-
LANCE);
02-483-7021 (DOCTOR)

VIETNAM   15 (AMBULANCE);
14 (FIRE); 13 (POLICE)

WALES   999

ZAMBIA   1-2-25067

ZIMBABWE   999 (GENERAL EMERGENCY);
994 (AMBULANCE);
993 (FIRE); 995 (POLICE)

OTHER NUMBERS
IN THE UNITED STATES:

POISON CONTROL CENTER
(800) 222-1222

ANIMAL POISON CONTROL CENTER
(888) 426-4435

CENTERS FOR DISEASE CONTROL
HOTLINE FOR INTERNATIONAL
TRAVELERS
(877) FYI-TRIP

TRAVEL ADVISORY WARNINGS
(US DEPT OF STATE)
(888) 407-4747

FBI HEADQUARTERS
(202) 324-3000

HELP FOR US CITIZENS ABROAD
(IN THE EVENT OF ARREST, DETENTION,
ROBBERY OR CRIME AGAINST US CITIZEN
ABROAD)
(888) 407-4747;
FROM OVERSEAS
(317) 472-2328

USE THESE CARDS TO COMMUNICATE BASIC NEEDS WHEN IN A FOREIGN COUNTRY. IF YOU NEED FURTHER ASSISTANCE, TURN TO PAGE 177 FOR USEFUL PICTOGRAMS.

INSTRUCTIONS: CUT ALONG DOTTED LINES AND PLACE THE APPROPRIATE CARD INTO YOUR WALLET, PURSE, OR BACK POCKET FOR EASY REFERENCE.

ENGLISH TO FRENCH

GOOD MORNING = BONJOUR

GOOD AFTERNOON = BONJOUR

HELLO = BONJOUR

GOOD EVENING = BONSOIR

GOODNIGHT = BONNE NUIT

GOODBYE = AU REVOIR

YES = OUI   NO = NON

THANK YOU = MERCI

YOU'RE WELCOME = DE RIEN

PLEASE = S'IL VOUS PLAIT

EXCUSE ME = PARDON

I DO NOT UNDERSTAND=JE NE COMPRENDS PAS

DO YOU SPEAK ENGLISH?=PARLEZ-VOUS ANGLAIS?

I DON'T SPEAK FRENCH=JE NE PARLE PAS FRANCAIS

ENGLISH TO GERMAN

GOOD MORNING = GUTEN MORGEN

GOOD DAY = GUTEN TAG

HELLO (TELEPHONE ONLY) = HALLO

GOOD EVENING = GUTEN ABEND

GOODNIGHT = GUTE NACHT

GOODBYE = AUF WIEDERSEHEN

YES = JA   NO = NEIN

THANK YOU = DANKE

YOU'RE WELCOME = BITTE

PLEASE = BITTE

EXCUSE ME = ENTSCHULDIGUNG

I DO NOT UNDERSTAND = ICH VERSTEHE NICHT

DO YOU SPEAK ENGLISH? = SPRECHEN SIE ENGLISCH?

I DON'T SPEAK GERMAN = ICH SPRECHE KEIN DEUTSCH

(NOTE: WS ARE PRONOUNCED WITH A "V" SOUND)

ENGLISH TO SPANISH

GOOD MORNING = BUENOS DIAS

GOOD AFTERNOON = BUENAS TARDES

HELLO = HOLA

GOOD EVENING = BUENAS NOCHES

GOODNIGHT = BUENAS NOCHES

GOODBYE = ADIÓS

YES = SÍ

NO = NO

THANK YOU = GRACIAS

YOU'RE WELCOME = DE NADA

PLEASE = POR FAVOR

EXCUSE ME = PERDÓN

I DO NOT UNDERSTAND = NO ENTIENDO

DO YOU SPEAK ENGLISH? = HABLA USTED INGLÉS?

I DON'T SPEAK SPANISH = NO HABLO ESPAÑOL

ENGLISH TO ITALIAN

GOOD MORNING = BUON GIORNO

GOOD AFTERNOON = BUON GIORNO

HELLO (FORMAL) = SALVE

GOOD EVENING = BUONA SERA

GOODNIGHT = BUONA NOTTE

GOODBYE = CIAO (INFORMAL) ARRIVEDERCI (FORMAL)

YES = SI

NO = NO

THANK YOU = GRAZIE

YOU'RE WELCOME = PREGO

PLEASE = PER FAVOR

EXCUSE ME = SCUSI

I DO NOT UNDERSTAND = NON CAPISCO

DO YOU SPEAK ENGLISH? = PARA INGLESE?

I DON'T SPEAK ITALIAN = NON PARLO ITALIANO

ENGLISH TO FRENCH

WHERE IS THE BATHROOM? = OÙ SONT LES TOILETTES?

WHERE IS . . .? = OÙ EST?

HOW MUCH? = C'EST COMBIEN?

ONE TICKET TO . . . = UN BILLET POUR . . .

NUMBERS:

ONE = UN

TWO = DEUX

THREE = TROIS

FOUR = QUATRE

FIVE = CINQ

SIX = SIX

SEVEN = SEPT

EIGHT = HUIT

NINE = NEUF

TEN = DIX

ENGLISH TO GERMAN

WHERE IS THE BATHROOM? = WO IST DIE TOILETTE?

WHERE IS . . .? = WO IST . . .?

HOW MUCH IS IT? = WIEVIEL KOSTET ES?

ONE TICKET TO . . . = EINE FAHRKARTE NACH . . .

NUMBERS:

ONE = EINS

TWO = ZWEI

THREE = DREI

FOUR = VIER

FIVE = FÜNF

SIX = SECHS

SEVEN = SIEBEN

EIGHT = ACHT

NINE = NEUN

TEN = ZEHN

ENGLISH TO SPANISH

WHERE IS THE BATHROOM? = ¿DÓNDE ESTÁ EL BAÑO?

WHERE IS . . .? = ¿DÓNDE ESTÁ?

HOW MUCH IS IT? = ¿CUÁNTO CUESTA?

ONE TICKET TO . . . = UN BOLETO PARA . . .

NUMBERS:

ONE = UNO

TWO = DOS

THREE = TRES

FOUR = CUATRO

FIVE = CINCO

SIX = SEIS

SEVEN = SIETE

EIGHT = OCHO

NINE = NUEVE

TEN = DIEZ

ENGLISH TO ITALIAN

WHERE IS THE BATHROOM? = DOVE LA TOLETTA?

WHERE IS . . .? = DOVE (PRONOUNCED "DOH-VEH")

HOW MUCH? = QUANTO?

ONE TICKET TO . . . = UN BIGLIETTO A . . .

NUMBERS:

ONE = UNO

TWO = DUE

THREE = TRE

FOUR = QUATTRO

FIVE = CINQUE

SIX = SEI

SEVEN = SETTE

EIGHT = OTTO

NINE = NOVE

TEN = DIECI

ENGLISH TO HEBREW

GOOD MORNING = BOKER TOV

GOOD AFTERNOON = TZOHORA'IM TOVIM

HELLO = SHALOM

GOOD EVENING = EREV TOV

GOODNIGHT = LILAH TOV   GOODBYE = SHALOM

YES = KEN   NO = LO

THANK YOU = TODA

YOU'RE WELCOME = BE'VAKASHA

PLEASE = BE'VAKASHA   EXCUSE ME = SLICHAH

I DO NOT UNDERSTAND = ANI LO MEVIN (MALE)

ANI LO MEVINAH (FEMALE)

DO YOU SPEAK ENGLISH? = ATA MEDABER ANGLIT? (M)

AT MEDABERET ANGLIT? (F)

I DON'T SPEAK HEBREW = ANI LO MEDABER IVRIT (M)

ANI LO MEDABERET IVRIT (F)

ENGLISH TO JAPANESE

GOOD MORNING = OHAYO GOZAIMASU

GOOD AFTERNOON = KONNICHIWA

HELLO = KONNICHIWA

GOOD EVENING = KONBANWA

GOODNIGHT = OYASUMINASAI

GOODBYE = SAYONARA

YES = HAI

NO = LIE

THANK YOU = ARIGATO

YOU'RE WELCOME = DO ITASHIMASHITE

PLEASE = DOZO

EXCUSE ME = SUMIMASEN

I DO NOT UNDERSTAND = WAKARIMASEN

DO YOU SPEAK ENGLISH? = EIGO GA DEKIMASU KA?

I DON'T SPEAK JAPANESE = NIHONGO GA DEKIMASEN

ENGLISH TO ARABIC

GOOD MORNING = SABAH AL-KHEIR

HELLO = MARHABA

GOOD EVENING = MASA' AL-KHEIR

GOODNIGHT = TISBAH AL-KHAYR

GOODBYE = MA' AS-SALAAMA

YES = AY-WAH   NO = LA

THANK YOU = SHUKRAN

YOU'RE WELCOME = AFWAN

PLEASE = MIN FADLAK (TO A MAN);

MIN FADLIK (TO A WOMAN)

EXCUSE ME = 'AN IZNAK (TO A MAN);

'AN IZNIK (TO A WOMAN)

I DO NOT UNDERSTAND = MA BAFHAM

DO YOU SPEAK ENGLISH? = BITIHKEE INGLIZI?

I DON'T SPEAK ARABIC = MA BIHKI ARABI

ENGLISH TO MANDARIN

GOOD MORNING = ZAO

GOOD AFTERNOON = NI HAO

HELLO = NI HAO

GOOD EVENING = NI HAO

GOODNIGHT = WAN AN

GOODBYE = ZAIJAIN

YES = SHI   NO = BU SHI

THANK YOU = XIE XIE

YOU'RE WELCOME = BU XIE

PLEASE = QING

EXCUSE ME = DUI BU QI

I DO NOT UNDERSTAND = WO BU MING BAI

DO YOU SPEAK ENGLISH? = NI HUI JIANG

YINGYU MA?

I DON'T SPEAK MANDARIN=WO BU HUI JIANG HUA YU

ENGLISH TO HEBREW

WHERE IS THE BATHROOM? = EIFO HA'SHERUTIM?

WHERE IS . . .? = EIFOH?

HOW MUCH? = KAHMAH?

ONE TICKET TO . . . = KARTIS ECHAD LE . . .

NUMBERS:

ONE = EH-HAD

TWO = SHTAYIM

THREE = SHALOSH

FOUR = ARBAH

FIVE = CHAMAYSH

SIX = SHAYSH

SEVEN = SHEVAH

EIGHT = SHMONEH

NINE = TAYSHAH

TEN = ESSER

ENGLISH TO JAPANESE

WHERE IS THE BATHROOM? = TOIRE WA DOKO DESU KA?

WHERE IS . . .? = WA DOKO DESU KA?

HOW MUCH? = IKURA DESU KA?

ONE TICKET TO . . . = KIPPU WO ICHIMAI ONEGAISHIMASU

NUMBERS:

ONE = ICHI

TWO = NI

THREE = SAN

FOUR = VON/SHI

FIVE = GO

SIX = ROKU

SEVEN = SHICHI/NANA

EIGHT = HACHI

NINE = KU/KYU

TEN = JU

ENGLISH TO ARABIC

WHERE IS THE BATHROOM? = WAYN BEYT ALMAY?

WHERE IS . . .? = WAYN . . .?

HOW MUCH IS THIS? = AH DESH HADAH?

ONE TICKET . . . = WAAHID TADHKARA . . .

NUMBERS:

ONE = WAAHID

TWO = TINEN

THREE = TALATAY

FOUR = ARBAHA

FIVE = KHAMSEH

SIX = SITTEH

SEVEN = SABAH

EIGHT = TAMANYEH

NINE = TAYSA

TEN = SHARAH

ENGLISH TO MANDARIN

WHERE IS THE TOILET? = XI SHOU JIAN ZAI NA LI

WHERE IS . . .? = ZAI NA LI . . .

HOW MUCH? = DUO SHAO

ONE TICKET TO . . . = YI ZHANG QU . . . DE PIAO

NUMBERS:

ONE = YI

TWO = ER

THREE = SAN

FOUR = SI

FIVE = WU

SIX = LIU

SEVEN = QI

EIGHT = BA

NINE = JIU

TEN = SHI

USE THESE PICTURES TO COMMUNICATE WITH PEOPLE WHO DON'T SPEAK YOUR LANGUAGE.

INSTRUCTIONS: POINT AT WHATEVER YOU ARE TRYING TO LOCATE OR BUY.

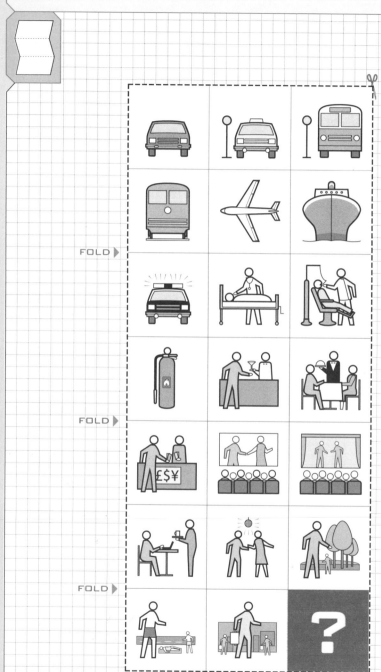

FOLD ▶

FOLD ▶

FOLD ▶

USE THIS CHART TO DETERMINE THE VALID CURRENCY IN YOUR TRAVELS.

INSTRUCTIONS: DETACH CHART AND STUDY WHILE TRAVELING.

CURRENCIES AROUND THE WORLD

AFGHANISTAN	AFGHANI
ALBANIA	LEK
ALGERIA	DINAR
ANDORRA	PESETA
ANGOLA	NEW KWANZA
ARGENTINA	PESO
ARUBA	FLORIN
AUSTRALIA	DOLLAR
BAHAMAS	DOLLAR
BAHRAIN	DINAR
BANGLADESH	TAKA
BARBADOS	DOLLAR
BELIZE	DOLLAR
BERMUDA	DOLLAR
BOTSWANA	PULA
BRAZIL	REAL
CHINA	YUAN
COLOMBIA	PESO
COSTA RICA	COLON
CROATIA	KUNA
CUBA	PESO
CZECH REPUBLIC	KORUNA
DENMARK	KRONE
DOMINICAN REPUBLIC	PESO
ECUADOR	SUCRE
EGYPT	POUND
EL SALVADOR	COLON
ETHIOPIA	BIRR
FRANCE	EURO (FORMERLY FRENCH FRANC)
GERMANY	EURO (FORMERLY DEUTSCHE MARK)
GHANA	CEDI
GREECE	EURO (FORMERLY DRACHMA)
GUATEMALA	QUETZAL
HAITI	GOURDE
HONDURAS	LEMPIRA
HONG KONG	DOLLAR

FOLD ACCORDIAN-STYLE FOR A HANDY WALLET-SIZE INSERT.

CURRENCIES AROUND THE WORLD

ICELAND	KRONA
INDIA	RUPEE
IRAN	RIAL
IRAQ	DINAR
ISRAEL	SHEKEL
ITALY	EURO (FORMERLY LIRA)
JAPAN	YEN
JORDAN	DINAR
KENYA	SHILLING
KUWAIT	DINAR
LITHUANIA	LITAS
MALAYSIA	RINGGIT
MEXICO	PESO
MONGOLIA	TUGRIK
MOROCCO	DIRHAM
THE NETHERLANDS	EURO (FORMERLY GUILDER)
NEPAL	RUPEE
NEW ZEALAND	DOLLAR
PAKISTAN	RUPEE
PANAMA	BALBOA
PERU	NUEVO SOL
POLAND	ZLOTY
PORTUGAL	EURO (FORMERLY ESCUDO)
ROMANIA	LEU
RUSSIA	RUBLE
SAUDI ARABIA	RIYAL
SOUTH AFRICA	RAND
SOUTH KOREA	WON
SPAIN	EURO (FORMERLY PESETA)
SWEDEN	KRONA
TAIWAN	N.T. DOLLAR
THAILAND	BAHT
UNITED KINGDOM	POUND STERLING
UNITED STATES	DOLLAR
VENEZUELA	BOLIVAR
VIETNAM	DONG
YUGOSLAVIA	DINAR
ZAMBIA	KWACHA

FOLD ▶

FOLD ▶

USE THIS GUIDE TO DOCUMENT YOUR EVENTUAL VISITS TO ALL THE WONDERS OF THE WORLD AND CHECK OFF AREAS ALREADY VISITED.

INSTRUCTIONS: DETACH GUIDE. CHECK OFF EACH AREA YOU VISIT. SEE PAGES 30 AND 177 FOR TRAVEL TIPS AND HELP.

WONDERS OF THE WORLD CHECKLIST

SEVEN WONDERS OF THE ANCIENT WORLD

☐ 1. THE HANGING GARDENS OF BABYLON (IRAQ)
☐ 2. THE GREAT PYRAMID OF GIZA (EGYPT)
☐ 3. THE LIGHTHOUSE OF ALEXANDRIA (EGYPT)
☐ 4. THE COLOSSUS OF RHODES (GREECE)
☐ 5. THE STATUE OF ZEUS (GREECE)
☐ 6. THE TEMPLE OF ARTEMUS (TURKEY)
☐ 7. THE MAUSOLEUM AT HALICARNASSUS (TURKEY)

SEVEN NATURAL WONDERS OF THE WORLD

☐ 1. GREAT BARRIER REEF (AUSTRALIA)
☐ 2. MOUNT EVEREST (NEPAL)
☐ 3. VICTORIA FALLS (ZIMBABWE/ZAMBIA)
☐ 4. HARBOR AT RIO DE JANEIRO (BRAZIL)
☐ 5. PARICUTIN VOLCANO (MEXICO)
☐ 6. GRAND CANYON (ARIZONA)
☐ 7. NORTHERN LIGHTS (ALASKA)

MODERN WONDERS OF THE WORLD

☐ 1. EIFFEL TOWER (PARIS, FRANCE)
☐ 2. ANGKOR WAT (CAMBODIA)
☐ 3. PANAMA CANAL (CENTRAL AMERICA)
☐ 4. THE TAJ MAHAL (INDIA)
☐ 5. THE LEANING TOWER OF PISA (ITALY)
☐ 6. THE STATUE OF LIBERTY (NEW YORK)
☐ 7. GREAT WALL OF CHINA (CHINA)

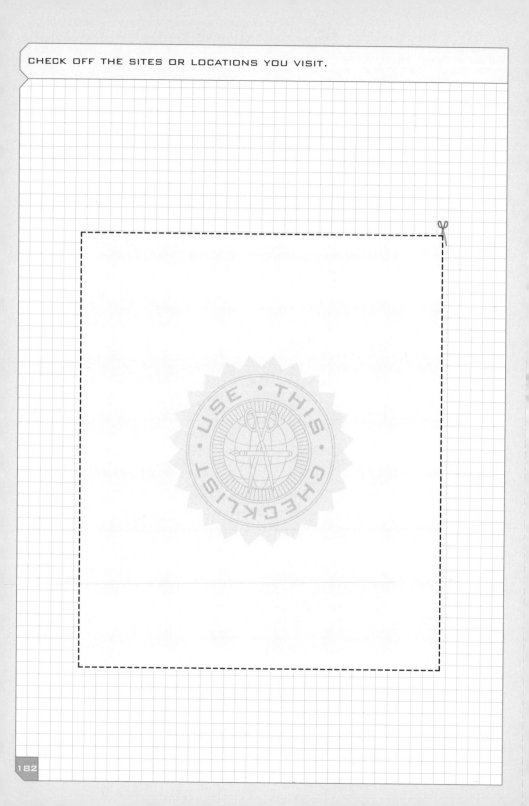

USE THIS CHART WHEN YOU NEED TO CONVERT DISTANCES AND MEASUREMENTS.

INSTRUCTIONS: CUT ALONG DOTTED LINES AND KEEP IN WALLET FOR EASY REFERENCE.

LENGTH ▶ INTO METRIC

IF YOU KNOW	MULTIPLY BY	TO GET
INCHES	2.54	CENTIMETERS
FOOT	.31	METERS
YARDS	0.91	METERS
MILES	1.6	KILOMETERS

MASS (WEIGHT) ▶ INTO METRIC

IF YOU KNOW	MULTIPLY BY	TO GET
OUNCES	28	GRAMS
POUNDS	.45	KILOGRAMS
SHORT TONS	0.9	METRIC TONS

VOLUME ▶ INTO METRIC

IF YOU KNOW	MULTIPLY BY	TO GET
TEASPOONS	5	MILLILITERS
TABLESPOONS	0.09	MILLILITERS
FLUID OUNCES	0.8	MILLILITERS
CUPS	2.6	LITERS
PINTS	0.4	LITERS
QUARTS	0.95	LITERS
GALLONS	3.8	LITERS
CUBIC FEET	0.03	CUBIC METERS
CUBIC YARDS	0.76	CUBIC METERS

AREA ▶ INTO METRIC

IF YOU KNOW	MULTIPLY BY	TO GET.
SQ. INCHES	6.5	SQ. CENTIMETERS
SQ. FEET	0.09	SQ. METERS
SQ. YARDS	0.8	SQ. METERS
SQ. MILES	2.6	SQ. KILOMETERS
ACRES	0.4	HECTARES

TEMPERATURE ▶ INTO CELSIUS

IF YOU KNOW	SUBTRACT	THEN MULTIPLY BY	TO GET
FAHRENHEIT	32	5/9	CELSIUS

SEE REVERSE SIDE FOR CONVERSIONS OUT OF METRIC

LENGTH ▶ OUT OF METRIC

IF YOU KNOW	MULTIPLY BY	TO GET
MILLIMETERS	0.04	INCHES
CENTIMETERS	0.4	INCHES
METERS	3.3	FEET
KILOMETERS	0.62	MILES

MASS (WEIGHT) ▶ OUT OF METRIC

IF YOU KNOW	MULTIPLY BY	TO GET
GRAMS	0.035	OUNCES
KILOGRAMS	2.2	POUNDS
METRIC TONS	1.1	SHORT TONS

◀ FOLD

VOLUME ▶ OUT OF METRIC

IF YOU KNOW	MULTIPLY BY	TO GET
MILLILITERS	0.03	FLUID OUNCES
LITERS	2.1	PINTS
LITERS	1.06	QUARTS
LITERS	0.26	GALLONS
CUBIC METERS	35	CUBIC FEET
CUBIC METERS	1.3	CUBIC YARDS
GALLONS	3.8	LITERS
CUBIC FEET	0.03	CUBIC METERS
CUBIC YARDS	0.76	CUBIC METERS

FOLD ▶

AREA ▶ OUT OF METRIC

IF YOU KNOW	MULTIPLY BY	TO GET
SQ. CENTIMETERS	0.16	SQ. INCHES
SQ. METERS	0.09	SQ. FEET
SQ. YARDS	1.2	SQ. YARDS
SQ. KILOMETERS	0.4	SQ. MILES
HECTARES	2.47	ACRES

TEMPERATURE ▶ INTO FAHRENHEIT

IF YOU KNOW	MULTIPLY BY	THEN ADD	TO GET
CELSIUS	9/5	32	FAHRENHEIT

SEE REVERSE SIDE FOR CONVERSIONS INTO METRIC

USE THIS CHART TO UNDERSTAND ROAD SIGNS WHEN IN EUROPE.

INSTRUCTIONS: DETACH PAGE AND CARRY WITH YOU WHEN YOU'RE DRIVING IN EUROPE.

EUROPEAN ROAD SIGNS

 TWO-WAY TRAFFIC

 RIGHT CURVE

 PRIORITY ROAD

 MERGING TRAFFIC

 PRIORITY ON RIGHT

 DANGEROUS CURVE

 DOUBLE CURVE

 ROAD NARROWS

 JUNCTION

 SLIPPERY ROAD

 CAUTION

 FALLING ROCKS

 PEDESTRIAN CROSSING

 MEN WORKING

 TRAFFIC JAM

 SIGNALS AHEAD

 YIELD

 TRAFFIC CIRCLE

 OPENING BRIDGE

 EMBANKMENT

 STEEP HILL

 RR XING—NO GATE

 RR XING WITH GATE

 ICE DANGER

 CROSSWIND

 ANIMAL CROSSING

 UNEVEN ROAD

 STOP

 STOP AT INTERSECTION

 NO ENTRY

EUROPEAN ROAD SIGNS

VEHICLES PROHIBITED

NO MOTOR VEHICLES

NO PEDESTRIANS

NO RIGHT TURN

NO U-TURN

NO PASSING

END/NO-PASSING ZONE

NO PASSING—TRUCKS

YIELD TO ONCOMING

PRIORITY TO LEFT

PRIORITY ROAD

END OF PRIORITY

DEAD END

WIDTH LIMIT

HEIGHT LIMIT

NO PARKING

NO PARKING on RIGHT

NO PARKING—ODD DAYS

NO STOPPING

SOFT SHOULDER

SPEED LIMIT

END of SPEED LIMIT

NATL. SPEED LIMIT APPLIES

BICYCLE LANE

BICYCLES PROHIBITED

ONE-WAY TRAFFIC

TURN AHEAD

KEEP LEFT

PARKING

HOSPITAL

USE THIS CHART TO DETERMINE THE LEGAL SPEED LIMIT WHERE YOU'RE DRIVING.

INSTRUCTIONS: DETACH PAGE AND KEEP WITH YOU IN YOUR ROAD TRAVELS.
NOTE: THESE SPEEDS MAY CHANGE, SO BE SURE TO ABIDE BY POSTED SIGNS.

DRIVING SPEED LIMITS AROUND THE WORLD

	HIGHWAY SPEED	REGULAR ROAD SPEED
AUSTRALIA	62–68 MPH (100–110 KM/HR)	37 MPH (60 KM/HR)
AUSTRIA	81 MPH (130 KM/HR)	62 MPH (99 KM/HR)
BELGIUM	75 MPH (120 KM/HR)	38 MPH (60 KM/HR)
CANADA	50–60 MPH (80–100 KM/HR)	31 MPH (50 KM/HR)
CZECH REPUBLIC	69 MPH (110 KM/HR)	38 MPH (60 KM/HR)
DENMARK	69 MPH (110 KM/HR)	44 MPH (70 KM/HR)
FRANCE	81 MPH (130 KM/HR)	55 MPH (90 KM/HR)
GERMANY	NONE	65 MPH (100 KM/HR)
GREECE	65 MPH (100 KM/HR)	38 MPH (60 KM/HR)
IRELAND	70 MPH (112 KM/HR)	50 MPH (80 KM/HR)
ITALY	81 MPH (130 KM/HR)	55 MPH (90 KM/HR)

	HIGHWAY SPEED	REGULAR ROAD SPEED
JAPAN	50 MPH (80 KM/HR)	25 MPH (40 KM/HR)
LUXEMBOURG	56-75 MPH (90-120 KM/HR)	34 MPH (55 KM/HR)
NEW ZEALAND	62 MPH (100KM/HR)	31 MPH (50 KM/H)
POLAND	69 MPH (110 KM/HR)	55 MPH (90 KM/HR)
PORTUGAL	65 MPH (100 KM/HR)	50 MPH (80 KM/HR)
SPAIN	75 MPH (120 KM/HR)	65 MPH (100 KM/HR)
SOUTH AFRICA	75 MPH (120 KM/HR)	34 MPH (55 KM/HR)
SWEDEN	69 MPH (110 KM/HR)	44 MPH (70 KM/HR)
SWITZERLAND	81 MPH (130 KM/HR)	38-50 MPH (60-80 KM/HR)
U.K.	70 MPH (112 KM/HR)	60 MPH (94 KM/HR)
USA	55-75 MPH (90-120 KM/HR)	15-45 MPH (24-72 KM/HR)

USE THIS DIAGRAM WHEN YOU NEED A QUICK LESSON IN DRIVING WITH A MANUAL TRANSMISSION (STICK SHIFT).

INSTRUCTIONS: DETACH DIAGRAM AND KEEP WITH YOU IN CASE YOU'RE REQUIRED TO DRIVE A STICK SHIFT (AND YOU DON'T ALREADY KNOW).

LEARN TO DRIVE A STICK SHIFT

1. IDENTIFY THE PEDALS:
   (FROM LEFT TO RIGHT) CLUTCH, BRAKE, GAS.

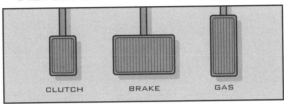

2. NOTICE HOW THE GEARSHIFT IS SET UP—MOST CARS USE AN "H" SHAPE WITH THE THIRD AND FIFTH GEARS AT THE TOPS; THE SECOND, FOURTH, AND REVERSE GEARS AT THE BOTTOM. THE CROSS BAR OF THE "H" IS NEUTRAL.

3. BE SURE THE PARKING BRAKE IS ON AND THE CAR IS ON A FLAT SURFACE.

4. PRESS YOUR LEFT FOOT DOWN ON THE CLUTCH AND MOVE THE GEARSHIFT TO NEUTRAL.

5. START THE CAR.

6. KEEPING THE CLUTCH PRESSED, PUT THE CAR INTO FIRST GEAR.

7. APPLY THE FOOT BRAKE WITH THE RIGHT FOOT; RELEASE THE PARKING BRAKE.

8. WHEN YOU ARE READY TO START DRIVING, RE-LEASE THE FOOT BRAKE (CLUTCH IS STILL PRESSED).

9. RELEASE THE CLUTCH SLOWLY UNTIL YOU HEAR THE ENGINE SLOW DOWN; THEN, PRESS ON THE GAS PEDAL WITH YOUR RIGHT FOOT AS YOU CONTINUE TO RELEASE THE CLUTCH. THE CAR WILL START TO MOVE FORWARD.

10. WHEN THE CAR HAS REACHED ABOUT 3,000 RPM, TAKE YOUR FOOT OFF THE GAS, PRESS DOWN ON THE CLUTCH, AND SWITCH TO SECOND GEAR.

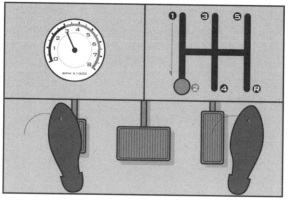

11. RELEASE THE CLUTCH AS YOU PRESS LIGHTLY ON THE GAS.

12. WHEN YOU HIT ANOTHER 3,000 RPM, SHIFT INTO HIGHER GEARS, FOLLOWING STEPS 10 THROUGH 11.

13. TO DOWNSHIFT (WHEN YOU WANT TO SLOW DOWN), RELEASE THE GAS PEDAL, PRESS DOWN ON THE CLUTCH, AND MOVE GEAR INTO NEUTRAL AND THEN THE NEXT LOWEST GEAR.

14. ONCE YOU'RE IN THE LOWER GEAR, RELEASE THE CLUTCH SLOWLY AND PRESS ON THE BRAKE.

15. TO STOP THE CAR, DOWNSHIFT INTO SECOND GEAR AND STEP ON THE BRAKE. APPLY THE CLUTCH JUST BEFORE THE CAR STOPS. DON'T DOWNSHIFT INTO FIRST.

TO DRIVE IN REVERSE: BEGIN WITH A STOPPED CAR. FOLLOW STEPS 6 THROUGH 9, PLACING THE GEARSHIFT INTO REVERSE. RELEASE THE CLUTCH EXTRA SLOWLY BECAUSE REVERSE GEAR ENGAGES FASTER. PRESS THE GAS PEDAL AS SOON AS THE CAR STARTS MOVING.

USE THIS CARD WHEN YOU NEED HELP CHANGING YOUR CAR'S TIRES.

INSTRUCTIONS: CUT OUT AT DOTTED LINES AND PUT IN THE GLOVE COMPARTMENT OF YOUR CAR FOR EASY REFERENCE.

HOW TO CHANGE A TIRE

YOU'LL NEED:
- JACK
- LUG WRENCH
- SPARE TIRE
- FLASHLIGHT (OPTIONAL)

STEPS:

1. MAKE SURE THE CAR IS ON A FLAT SUR-FACE AND AWAY FROM TRAFFIC. (DO NOT CHANGE A TIRE ON AN INCLINE!) TURN ON YOUR HAZARD LIGHTS.

2. REMOVE THE HUBCAP IF APPLICABLE.

3. USING A LUG WRENCH, LOOSEN THE LUG NUTS (DON'T REMOVE THEM).

4. POSITION THE JACK UNDER THE CAR. (YOUR OWNER'S MANUAL WILL SPECIFY WHERE YOUR JACK NEEDS TO BE POSITIONED.)

5. USING THE JACK, RAISE THE CAR UNTIL THE TIRE IS ABOUT A HAND'S SPAN OFF THE GROUND.

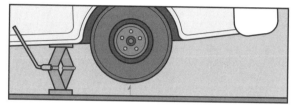

6. REMOVE THE LUG NUTS AND PUT THEM ASIDE CAREFULLY. REMOVE THE TIRE.

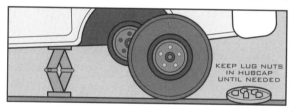

KEEP LUG NUTS IN HUBCAP UNTIL NEEDED

7. PUT ON THE SPARE TIRE (PUSH IT ONTO THE AXLE UNTIL IT CANNOT GO ANY FARTHER).

8. REPLACE THE LUG NUTS AND TIGHTEN THEM EVENLY BUT NOT FULLY; GO FAR ENOUGH TO HOLD THE TIRE IN PLACE WHILE YOU LOWER THE CAR.

9. LOWER THE CAR USING THE JACK.

10. TIGHTEN THE LUG NUTS IN A STAR FASHION, SO THAT YOU ALWAYS TIGHTEN THE ONE OPPOSITE FROM THE ONE YOU'VE JUST TIGHTENED. (THIS ENSURES THE TIRE IS IN PLACE EVENLY.)

NOTE: MOST SPARE TIRES ARE IDENTICAL TO YOUR OTHER TIRES; SOME TIRES, CALLED "DONUTS," ARE ONLY MEANT TO BE USED IN EMERGENCIES (E.G., TO DRIVE THE CAR TO THE SHOP).

USE THIS CUP WHEN YOU NEED SOMETHING TO HOLD YOUR WATER.

INSTRUCTIONS:
CUT OUT THE DIAGRAM ALONG THE DOTTED LINES.
FOLD THE PAPER IN HALF DIAGONALLY [1] AND POSITION THE FOLDED EDGE TOWARD YOU.
FOLD EACH SIDE [2-3] OVER AS SHOWN.
FOLD THE TRIANGULAR PART AT THE TOP [4] TOWARD YOU AND OVER THE FRONT OF THE CUP.
FOLD TRIANGULAR PART AT THE BACK [5] DOWN AND OVER THE BACK OF THE CUP (SEE DIAGRAM ON REVERSE SIDE OF THIS PAGE.)

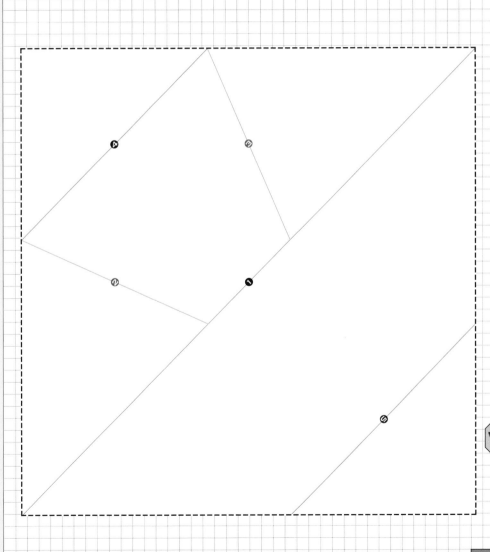

USE THESE COASTERS TO PROTECT YOUR HOME FURNISHINGS FROM DAMAGE.

INSTRUCTIONS: CUT OUT COASTERS ALONG DOTTED LINES. DECORATE AS DESIRED WITH WATERPROOF OR PERMANENT MEDIA.

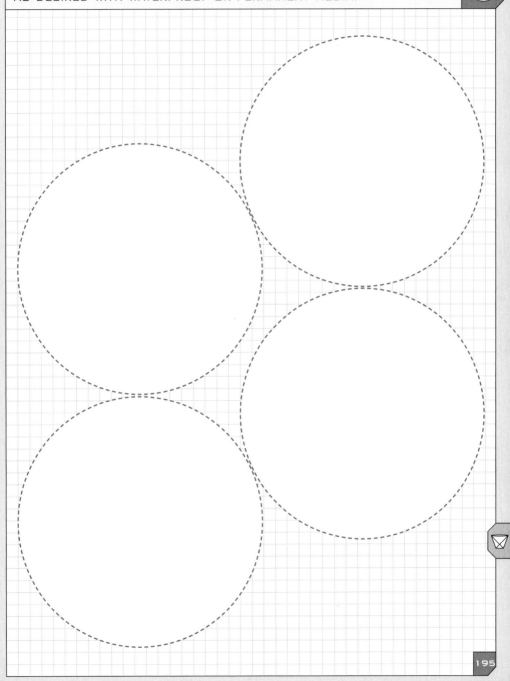

USE THIS FAN TO KEEP COOL IN WARM TEMPERATURES.

INSTRUCTIONS: CUT OUT FAN ALONG DOTTED LINES. FOLD AS
INDICATED. (SEE DIAGRAM ON REVERSE SIDE OF THIS PAGE.)

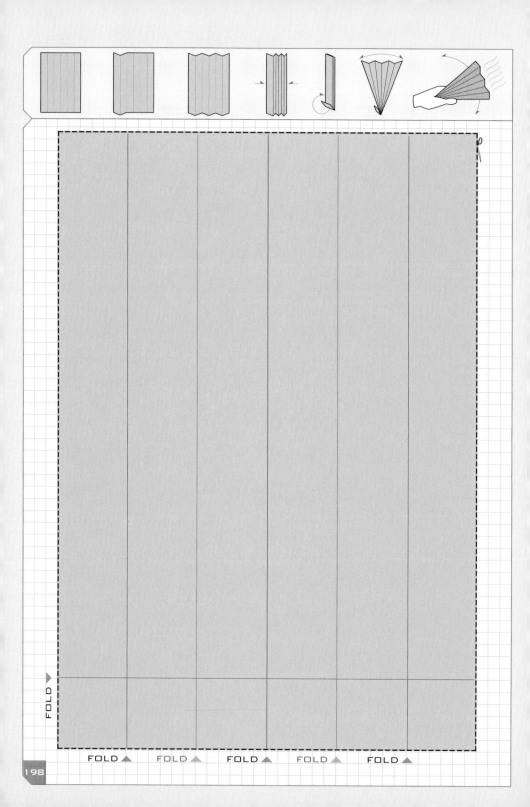

FOLD ▼

FOLD ▲   FOLD ▲   FOLD ▲   FOLD ▲   FOLD ▲

USE THESE TAGS TO IDENTIFY YOUR BAGS WHILE TRAVELING.

INSTRUCTIONS: WRITE PHONE NUMBER ON CARD. (NOTE: DO NOT WRITE NAME AND ADDRESS OR YOUR PERSONAL INFORMATION WILL BE AVAILABLE TO ANYONE WHO FINDS YOUR BAG.) STAPLE A RUBBER BAND (NOT INCLUDED) TO TAG, FOLD AS INDICATED, AND ATTACH TO LUGGAGE WITH RUBBER BAND.

INSERT PANEL A INTO RUBBER BAND, FOLD PANEL OVER BAND, AND STAPLE

IF FOUND, PLEASE CALL

PHONE NUMBER

IF FOUND, PLEASE CALL

PHONE NUMBER

IF FOUND, PLEASE CALL

PHONE NUMBER

IF FOUND, PLEASE CALL

PHONE NUMBER

FOLD PANEL B UNDER STAPLED PANEL A TO CLOSE TAG

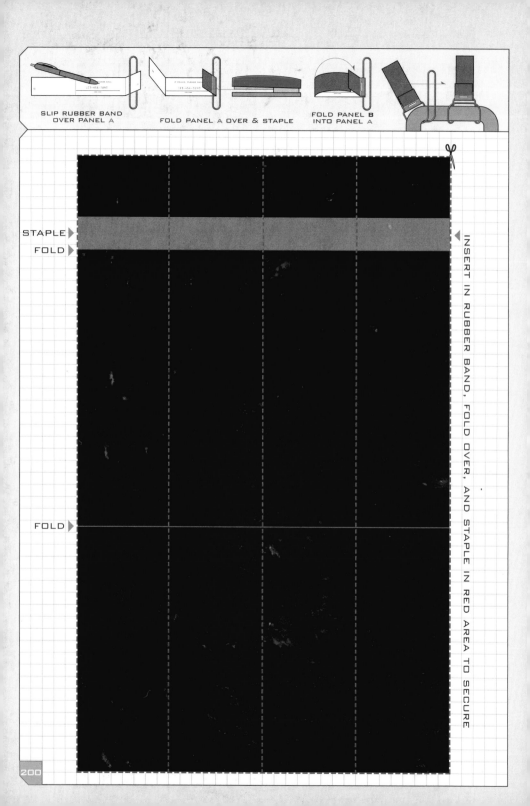

SLIP RUBBER BAND
OVER PANEL A

FOLD PANEL A OVER & STAPLE

FOLD PANEL B
INTO PANEL A

STAPLE ▶

FOLD ▶

FOLD ▶

INSERT IN RUBBER BAND, FOLD OVER, AND STAPLE IN RED AREA TO SECURE

USE THIS POSTCARD WHEN YOU'RE TRAVELING IN THE UNITED STATES AND WANT TO SEND NOTES BACK TO THOSE YOU LOVE.

INSTRUCTIONS: FILL OUT THE FRONT OF THE POSTCARD ACCORDING TO LOCATION. CUT OUT ALONG DOTTED LINE, ADDRESS, STAMP, AND SEND.

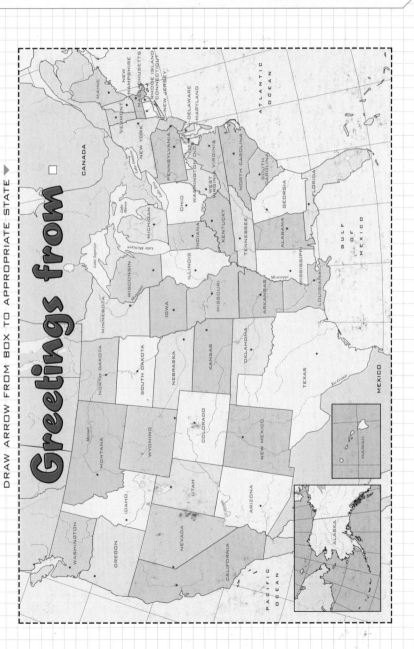

DRAW ARROW FROM BOX TO APPROPRIATE STATE ▶

Greetings from □

USE THIS POSTCARD

PLACE
STAMP
HERE

USE THIS POSTCARD WHEN YOU'RE TRAVELING WORLDWIDE AND WANT TO SEND NOTES BACK TO THOSE YOU LOVE.

INSTRUCTIONS: FILL OUT THE FRONT OF THE POSTCARD ACCORDING TO LOCATION. CIRCLE OR INDICATE WITH AN "X" THE APPROPRIATE COUNTRY ON THE MAP. CUT OUT, ADDRESS, STAMP, AND SEND.

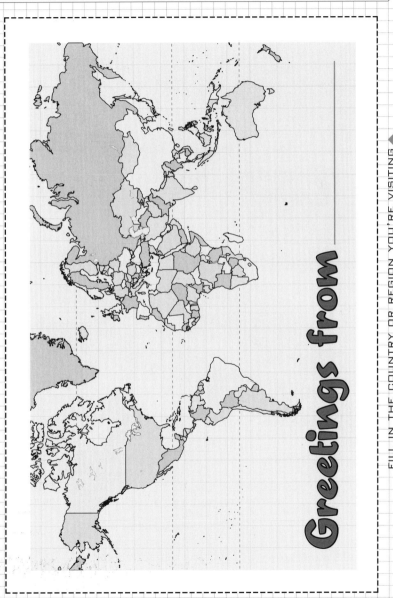

Greetings from

FILL IN THE COUNTRY OR REGION YOU'RE VISITING ▲

USE THIS POSTCARD

PLACE
STAMP
HERE

USE THESE LABELS TO IDENTIFY SEEDS THAT YOU'VE PLANTED IN YOUR GARDEN.

INSTRUCTIONS: CUT LABELS OUT ALONG DOTTED LINES. WITH PERMANENT MARKER, WRITE THE TYPE OF PLANT AND PLANTING DATE. STICK INTO SOIL WITH POINTED END DOWN.

PLANT: _____ DATE: _____

PLANT: _____ DATE: _____

PLANT: _____ DATE: _____

PLANT: _____ DATE: _____

PLANT: _____ DATE: _____

PLANT: _____ DATE: _____

USE THIS MASK AS A LAST-MINUTE COSTUME FOR A MASQUERADE OR HALLOWEEN PARTY.

INSTRUCTIONS: CUT THE MASK AND EYES OUT ALONG THE DOTTED LINES. DECORATE AS DESIRED. TAPE A PENCIL (NOT INCLUDED) TO THE INSIDE OF THE MASK (AS ILLUSTRATED ON THE NEXT PAGE). YOU CAN ALSO POKE HOLES ON THE SIDES AND SECURE IT WITH STRING.

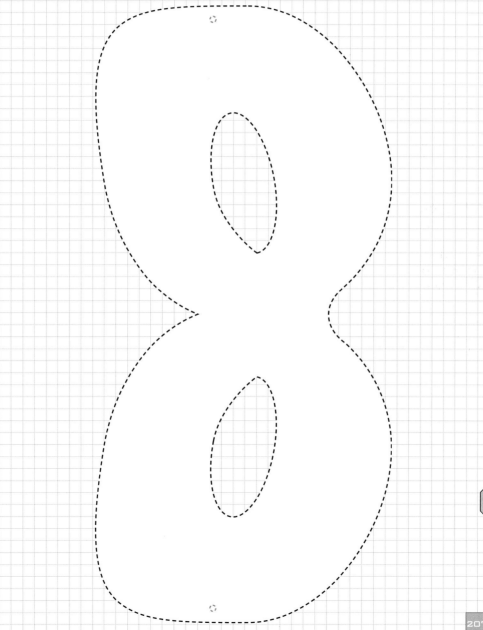

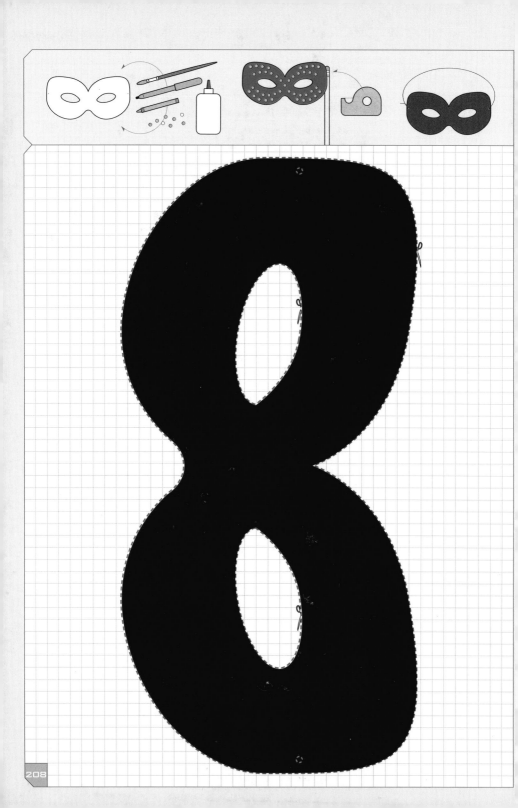